PAKISTAN'S ECONOMIC AND SOCIAL DEVELOPMENT

The Domestic, Regional and Global Context

S. Akbar Zaidi

Rupa . Co

in association with
OBSERVER RESEARCH FOUNDATION

Published by
Rupa . Co
7/16, Ansari Road, Daryaganj,
New Delhi 110 002

Sales Centres:

Allahabad Bangalore Chandigarh
Chennai Hyderabad Jaipur Kathmandu
Kolkata Mumbai Pune

Typeset in 11 pt. Classical Garamond by
Nikita Overseas Pvt Ltd
1410 Chiranjiv Tower,
43 Nehru Place
New Delhi 110 019

Printed in India by
Saurabh Printers Pvt Ltd,
A-16, Sector-IV,
Noida 201 301

Contents

Acknowledgements

This monograph was first presented at the Observer Research Foundation in New Delhi on February 23, 2004, before a large audience which offered numerous comments on the first draft. The Observer Research Foundation had also commissioned eight Indian academics, journalists and policy makers to give more detailed, written comments. I am grateful to all the participants at the presentation, in particular to Sushant Sareen, Professor Yoginder Alag, Professor Suresh Tendulkar, Professor Arjun Sengupta, Dr Charan Wadhva, Dr V.R. Panchmukhi, Dr Surjit Bhalla, T.N. Ninan and Dr Sanjaya Baru, for their very substantial and detailed comments. This final publication incorporates a large number of the comments made by all those who participated in the discussion.

Introduction

In a world which is increasingly globalised and competitive, economic growth and social development depend on how countries relate to the rest of the world and on the economic policies that they follow. Apart from the more standard requirements of adequate capital and skilled labour, other factors that have gained importance in explaining economic development and growth, increasingly include include non-economic criteria, such as the quality of governance in countries, how their institutions function, and openness and transparency in society, often reflected through the depth of democracy in that country. With often dramatically changing regional and global political circumstances, not least in the countries that constitute and are near South Asia, economic prospects are increasingly associated with issues of war, peace and global coalitions and alliances. As a consequence, economic development has increasingly become a matter of *political* economy.

Compared to other countries in South Asia, perhaps, Pakistan has experienced a far greater degree of political drama in the last decade. With governments since 1985 changing every few months, with no democratically elected government being allowed to complete its tenure since elections resumed in 1985, the economic consequences have been quite noticeable, leaving an imprint on social development and society at large. In the short period since 1998, however, even Pakistan's unsettled political path has received some serious jolts. Both domestically and most certainly regionally, the period since 1998 has been one of the most extraordinary in the country's 57-year history, and this has had profound repercussions on the economy as well.

The purpose of this monograph is to illustrate, document and analyse the direction of Pakistan's development since 1947, with a greater focus on the period since the 1980s, and especially on the last few years. We provide data and offer interpretations and explanations of why the economy has developed the way it has, what the main features of that development have been, and try to identify successes and failures as a consequence of that development. With numerous disjunctures and discontinuities in the domestic political process, we look at how different governments and eras have left their imprint on the economic map, and how their relations with international organisations and global and regional powers have affected economic progress. We highlight key features that have come to shape Pakistan's economy, and as a consequence affected its political structure as well.

In order to focus more on the *issues* in Pakistan's economy rather than on developments related to individual leaders or eras, our format follows a thematic/issues approach rather than one which provides a linear narrative from the early days after Partition. Nevertheless, each of the issues discussed does have an historic account which also reflects developments in the past. We begin with a description of the structure of Pakistan's economy and compare it to the situation five decades earlier, in order to capture the degree and nature of change that has taken place. We then discuss the five eras of development in Pakistan, providing a broad overview of the political eras since 1947, together with some information on each period. This section, too, captures a flavour of the course of events spanning nearly six decades, highlighting key economic developments during Pakistan's history.[1]

We then move on to analysing the important sectors and issues that have emerged in recent years and have a bearing on Pakistan's current and future social condition. Beginning with the issues related to Pakistan's social development and the emergence of poverty as a serious problem, we compare

1. The periodisation of any economy is subject to some degree of subjectivity and hence, open to question. Many analysts avoid a political periodisation of growth since growth trends cannot be split by change of government as there is a continuation of prior growth trends. Also, if policies stay the same, periodisation is also problematic if governments keep changing at frequent intervals, as was the case in Pakistan. Nevertheless, it has become convention in analysing Pakistan's economic performance to break the 57 years down into blocks associated with the nature of the regime, a convention that we follow.

Pakistan with other countries, including those in South Asia. Pakistan has struggled with a domestic and external debt problem which has constrained the country's ability to develop at a higher level. Since it has to make high interest repayments annually, very little has been left over for development.

The implications of globalisation are discussed, as are the structural reforms that have taken place since the late 1980s. Given the critical role of Pakistan's neighbours and of the region as a whole on its developments, we examine Pakistan's position within South Asia, and look at the extent and possibilities of building further economic links, particularly with India. Finally, we look at some of the most recent developments that have taken place in and around Pakistan since 1998, which have had a considerable bearing on the economy as well.

The Structure of the Economy

Probably the most striking feature that is manifested in a view of Pakistan in 2004 compared to 1947, is that Pakistan today is less than half of what it was in 1947. In 1949-50, fifty-five per cent of Pakistan's population lived in the then East Pakistan, making it the majority province in terms of population. Despite this majority, economically the eastern wing was discriminated against and exploited. A section of the ruling elite of the western wing of Pakistan became the oppressor and exploiter of the East Pakistani people, leading to their eventual secession after a long and painful war of liberation ending in 1971.

The contribution made by East Pakistan to Pakistan's economy and society was huge, though never fully recognised or appreciated by West Pakistanis. Hence the first and perhaps most striking feature of Pakistan, a fact which many born after 1971 no longer consider, is that Pakistan today is half of what it was in 1947. Nevertheless, no matter how significant this loss, post-1971 Pakistan seems to have moved on from the first twenty-five of its 57-years. In fact, the first 57 years of Pakistan's history are conspicuously broken into two eras, which stand for the formation of two separate countries.

In 1947, Pakistan had every right to be called an 'agricultural' country. Most observers not fully cognisant with structural changes that have taken place in recent years, make the serious mistake of still calling Pakistan an agricultural country even after nearly six decades, when there is little reason to do so. At the time of Independence, the major share of (West) Pakistan's[1] Gross Domestic Product was from agriculture, which contributed around 53 per cent, compared to the 7.8 per cent from manufacturing and 11.9 per cent from retail trade. More than 65 per cent of Pakistan's labour force worked in agriculture, and almost all of Pakistan's exports consisted of primary products, essentially agricultural commodities like jute and tea which, not surprisingly, originated from East Pakistan (see Table 1).

The extent of change in Pakistan's economic structure as seen from Table 1, shows that in 2004, agriculture contributes a mere 23.6 per cent towards GDP, while manufacturing is up to 18.4 per cent. The services sector has replaced agriculture as the dominant sector in the economy, contributing more than half of total GDP. The population employed in agriculture has also fallen, although at around 48 per cent of the total labour force, agriculture is still the biggest sector in terms of the employed labour force.

---

1. All data refer to (West) Pakistan.

More importantly, the nature of exports from Pakistan have also changed dramatically. From 99.3 per cent of total exports in 1947, primary commodities now constitute around 11 per cent only. However, one must emphasise the fact that although 77 per cent of Pakistan's exports are now manufactured goods, with textiles, garments and yarn making up most of the exports, these figures are less impressive when we realise that much of these exports still depend critically on raw cotton.

Despite this dependence, one cannot strictly call Pakistan a 'one crop' (cotton) country since the value added share of wheat is almost identical to that of cotton (30 percent), followed by rice (17 percent), sugarcane (16 percent) and other minor crops (17 percent). In addition, with the increase in wheat production over recent years, Pakistan has also become self-sufficient in wheat and the issue of food security has, for some years to come, been addressed.

These economic changes in structure are also manifested in where people live. In 1951 when the first census in independent Pakistan was held, only 17 per cent of West Pakistanis lived in areas designated as urban; today estimates suggest that far more than 40 per cent live in cities and towns. This shift has major repercussions which affect the economy, society and the current political process. In fact, in the context of Pakistan, perhaps the most important political factor over the last few decades has been the process and extent of urbanisation and the emergence, and perhaps consolidation, of a middle class.

Table 1: Pakistan Basic Facts 1947-2004

Pakistan is the world's sixth most populous country and has the 44th biggest economy in terms of GDP; while using Purchasing Power Parity figures, Pakistan is the 28th largest economy. However, it is 164th out of 203 nations in terms of per capita GDP, and the 144th out of 190 countries in terms of the Human Development Index

Population (mn)	**33.78 (1951)**	**150 (2004)**
Urban (%)	17.8	40
Contribution to GDP	**1949-50**	**2002-03**
Agriculture	53.2	23.6
Manufacturing (incl. construction, elec. & gas)	7.8	25.7
Services and Trade	39.0	50.7
Labour Force by sector (%)	**1950-51**	**2003-04**
Agriculture	65.3	48.42
Manufacturing	9.5	18.03
Services and Trade	25.2	33.55
GNP per capita $	170 (1976)	440 (2000)
PPP GDP per capita $	820 (1960)	1928 (2000)
Composition of exports (%)	**1951-52**	**2002-03**
Primary Commodities	99.2	11
Semi-manuf		12
Manufacturers		77
Literacy rate (%)	15 (1951)	42 (2002-03)
Female literacy	12	29

Source: S. Akbar Zaidi, *Issues in Pakistan's Economy* (revised and up-dated second edition), Oxford University Press, 2004.

With more than 40 per cent of the country's population living in cities and towns, the economic profile, in terms of consumption and production patterns, has also changed quite drastically, and again, the cliché that 'Pakistan is mainly an agricultural economy', is no longer true. Urbanisation's impact on social and economic development is also very significant, and the extent and process of urbanisation was considered to be an indicator of progress and modernisation. Although many latter-day modernisers and developmentalists may no longer hold that that assumption is true, one cannot overlook the significant structural change that has been brought about by the process of urbanisation in fifty years. While only 6 million inhabitants out of a population of 33.8 million in 1947 were residing in towns and cities, now more than ten times that number do so. This figure is bound to be larger since there is now consensus amongst social scientists that a huge proportion of Pakistan is part of the urban economy and urban culture.[2]

Just as the cliché that 'Pakistan is an agricultural country', is repeated ad nauseum by analysts of the country's economy, another myth which prevails and is related to this is that 'Pakistan is a feudal country'. No matter how one looks at the facts and observes the manner in which society has evolved, there is no justification for believing, let alone repeating, what is perhaps Pakistan's most popular myth. There is no evidence to support this assertion. The Green Revolution of the sixties,

---

2. Some analysts suggest that Pakistan is now almost completely urban with so-called 'rural' areas fully integrated into the overall urban economy. See the excellent work by Reza Ali, in Zaidi, S. Akbar (ed), *Continuity and Change: Socio-political and Institutional Dynamics in Pakistan*, City Press, Karachi, 2003.

with its extraordinary impact on the rural areas, agriculture, the economy, and on the social relations of production, put an end once and for all to the myth that Pakistan is a 'feudal' country.

Key indicators and trends suggest that Pakistan's agriculture has moved on to capitalist lines. For example, in the case of the share of marketable surplus produced by farms and agricultural units, a huge majority of farms produce primarily for the market, not for self-consumption – in the early 1950s around 12 per cent of the produce was marketed, a figure which is now closer to 80 percent;[3] there has been a marked decline of sharecropping being replaced by wage labour; the size of holdings has fallen sharply forcing owners to run farms for profit through production for the market using modern technology; there has been a noticeable shift towards cash crops and fruits, and orchards are now seen as viable economic units; commercial, market-oriented farming dominates all forms of agricultural production.

Feudalism is no longer an economically viable and feasible project at the farm/landlord level, and many a 'feudal lord' has had to become a capitalist farmer or has then turned to other sources of income. While feudalism in Pakistan died a very long time ago, modern day Pakistan has seen the demise of agriculturists as a powerful economic, social and political force. The old social structures associated with feudals have also been replaced with a market dominated form of existence –

3. I am grateful to Professor Mahmood Hasan Khan for giving me this information.

agriculture is capitalist

particularly free and mobile labour – something which also explains the rise in poverty in rural areas, discussed in a separate section later. The huge change in economic, social and hence, political power, from the agriculturist, so-called feudal, lobby, towards an urban and rural middle class, is also one of the key indicators highlighting extraordinary structural change in Pakistan in nearly six decades.

While a growing number of people (including analysts and academics) in Pakistan are increasingly accepting the view that the power of the 'feudals' – both political and very certainly economic – has considerably declined on account of demographic and economic structural change and has been replaced by a mix and variety of middle class elements, it seems strange that the perception that 'Pakistan is feudal' still prevails outside Pakistan, particularly in India. Perhaps the lack of any democratic culture in Pakistan and the fact that the position of women is particularly discriminatory and shameful, gives rise to this impression. Also, while feudalism as a mode of production has dissipated, this does not mean that oppression and exploitation at the local/micro level has vanished.

What is being emphasised here is that while there are pockets of 'feudal' tendencies still prevalent in Pakistan, feudalism as a dominating and organising form of social and economic structure is no longer present. While Pakistan still has to develop a modern, democratic and socially responsible middle class and culture, the absence of this social group does not imply the presence of feudalism. With changes in land-holding and the rise of the *arthi* and transporter as key economic

why impression is feudalism

and political figures in rural areas, and with inheritance laws breaking large land-holdings, the old power structures based on land have changed conspicuously.[4]

---

4. For anyone interested in researching the feudalism argument in the case of Pakistan further, please see Chapter 2 in Zaidi, S. Akbar, *Issues in Pakistan's Economy* (revised and up-dated, second edition), Oxford University Press, 2004.

Macro-economic Growth: Five Decades and Five Epochs

The fifty-seven years since 1947 can be distinguished by at least five (with perhaps a sixth now emerging) specific epochs or eras which represent different economic policies, and planning and management choices. The first eleven years, between 1947-58, are the years when the country and economy were trying to settle down, but to no avail. This period was followed by what many still call the golden era of economic development (or at least economic growth) in the Decade of Development under Ayub Khan. The economy and the political scene had indeed stabilised and settled down with a consequence that growth rates were unprecedented, and Pakistan was considered to be one of the few countries at that time which would achieve developed-country status.

The *New York Times* of 18 January 1965 stated: 'Pakistan may be on its way toward an economic milestone reached by only one other populous country, the United States'; the

London *Times* echoed this sentiment on 26 February 1966 saying that, 'the survival and development of Pakistan is one of the most remarkable examples of state and nation building in the post-war period.' However, with the war of liberation in East Pakistan, the majority wing left Pakistan to form Bangladesh and two, not one, new countries were born.[1]

Post-1971 Pakistan was a new country in every respect, in comparison to the one that existed between 1947 and 1971. The third brief, albeit highly significant era in Pakistan's history, was the five-and-a-half years of Zulfiqar Ali Bhutto. His populism or Islamic Socialism – or just plain rhetoric – made him the most popular, and at that time, only elected leader to emerge in what was left of Pakistan. His rule ended by the imposition of Pakistan's second martial law under General Zia ul Haq in 1977. There were some similarities between the first and the second martial laws, but the world was now a different place compared to that of the 1960s. The opening up of the Middle East, the Afghan war with its consequences of a drug and arms culture in Pakistan, attempts at the Islamisation of the economy and society, and a praetorian sort of democracy between 1985-88, were amongst the salient features of the Zia era.

The death of General Zia in many ways brought about the end of the old Pakistan and 1988, with the rebirth of democracy, signals the third birth of the nation following the two earlier

1. Some of the historical narrative in this publication is drawn from Zaidi, S. Akbar, *Issues in Pakistan's Economy* (revised and up-dated, second edition), Oxford University Press, 2004.

ones, in 1947 and 1971. While political and social changes were emerging fast, the post-1988 economic changes and programmes also represented a departure from the past with very significant impacts on society, many of which were highly deleterious. However, in 1999, once again Pakistan was set off on yet another trajectory, in many ways an attempt to undo the Zia legacy further.

Laying the Foundations: 1947-58

In 1947 Pakistan was, indeed, a predominantly agrarian, undeveloped, newly independent nation, with little industry, few services and no infrastructure. In the first few years, Pakistan's main concern was survival; adverse international conditions and a precarious domestic situation, with millions of refugees, made the provision of very basic necessities the primary task of the government. Attempts to restructure the economy and to ensure that it was on a strong footing could only have been undertaken after the initial political and economic needs of the country were dealt with.

The first decade of economic policy and planning witnessed the attempts of a bureaucracy trying to keep Pakistan on its feet. The herculean task of building an economic base was left to the state sector as the private sector was still in its embryonic stages and did not have the capital to lead an industrial revolution in the country. It was the windfall gain made by the mercantile class during and after the Korean war in 1952 that paved the way for the foundations of industry, which the state sector helped develop and then handed over to the private sector.

The Decade of Development: 1958-68

If we examine Pakistan's economic growth record, the decade of the 1960s stands out as the best performer. Table 2 gives a useful indication of the nature of the differences between the decades of the sixties, seventies, eighties and nineties. While the rates of growth for the 1960s and the 1980s do seem to be quite close in most categories, there are important conceptual and ideological differences in the modes of development under the two military regimes.

Table 2: Growth Rates (%)

	GDP	Agriculture	Manufacturing	Services
1950s	3.1	1.6		
1960s	6.8	5.1	9.9	6.7
1970s	4.8	2.4	5.5	6.3
1980s	6.5	5.4	8.2	6.7
1990s	4.6	4.4	5.8	4.6
1990-91 to 1995-96	5.0	4.2	5.2	5.1
1995-96 to 1999-2000	4.0	4.9	3.2	4.0
1999-2000	3.6	0.4	7.0	4.8
2000-01	2.2	-2.7	8.2	4.8
2001-02	3.4	-0.1	5.0	4.1
2002-03	5.1	4.1	7.7	5.3

Source: Government of Pakistan, *Pakistan Economic Survey*, various issues, Islamabad.

Dozens of economists and social scientists have written on Ayub Khan's era and they are generally agreed that considerable economic growth and development did indeed take place. They argue that significant leaps were made in industrial and agricultural production, where growth rates in excess of 20 per cent per annum were witnessed in the large scale manufacturing sector. In the first five years of the Ayub period, manufacturing grew by as much as 17 per cent, and in the second half of Ayub Khan's reign, agricultural growth increased by 6 per cent, while industry grew by 10 per cent. Table 2 shows that the economy in general, and the different individual sectors, grew by phenomenal rates and Pakistan was considered to be a model capitalist economy in the 1960s.

Observers have pointed out that this aggressive capitalist development caused serious economic, social and political tensions. They argued that there was increased disparity in incomes across different regions. This was manifest in the concentration of economic prosperity in both the industrial and agricultural sectors in central Punjab, and in industry in Karachi. Critics of Ayub Khan's model of development point out that these two regions were permitted to grow at the expense of the rest of the country and the end result was the feeling of utter neglect and betrayal in the region of East Pakistan. Apart from the very obvious phenomenon of regional disparities, a number of scholars also took great pains to show that there was a great deal of economic concentration amongst individuals and numerous business empires were created. This resulted in increasing income inequality.

Of course, all this did happen. There was tremendous growth, but there was also increasing disparity across class and region. The social sectors were also neglected. There was little or no increase in the level of real wages, and social equity was of little concern. Functional inequality was the preferred philosophy of Mahbub-ul-Haq and Ayub Khan's Harvard Advisory Group, and their focus was on the rich, who were supposed to generate more savings, and thus were to be the motors of capitalist growth and development. The consequence of Ayub Khan's economic policies was that there was growth, development, the forces of production did expand, a proletariat was born; compared to the earlier periods, this was indeed a very progressive era in the evolution of the economic and political process in Pakistan.

However, what is most interesting about Ayub Khan's era is the fact that the economic package was thoroughly *illiberal* and was almost the opposite of what is being termed economic liberalism today. It was capitalism, and the private sector did play a significant role, but it was guided, governed and directed by the bureaucracy. The bureaucracy played an active, influential, and constructive role in the establishment of private sector capital in Pakistan. Dozens of constraints on setting up industry, red tape and numerous hurdles in financial and industrial policy did not stop the impressive growth in this period.

The nature of the economy was precisely what it should not have been according to the doctrine of economic liberalism and liberalisation fashionable today. Trade was highly controlled. The exchange rate was overvalued and it distorted local markets. Financial capital was rationed, and the stock market was a playground for a handful of people. The government's presence was everywhere, directing and encouraging the private sector and the market. The agricultural sector was consciously identified by the government as a vehicle for growth and numerous (governmental) decisions were taken which resulted in impressive growth, at times in excess of 11 per cent per year. The agricultural sector was transformed from a pre-capitalist to a capitalist one, only due to the active involvement and interference by the state. The private sector could not have flourished without the government, where even public sector projects commissioned by the Pakistan Industrial Development Corporation were gifted away to the private sector. The bureaucracy, in essence, gave birth to the private sector capitalist in Pakistan. Indeed, a very illiberal process according to conventional wisdom.

The Years of Bad Luck: 1971-77

Ironically, while most intellectuals condemned Ayub Khan's policies, it was these policies which gave rise to populism and the brand of policies particular to Zulfiqar Ali Bhutto, who was supported by the same intellectuals. Without Ayub, Bhutto would not have been possible. Bhutto's economic policies were more illiberal than those of his predecessor and his nationalisation was said to be the major cause for a huge downward trend in growth. However, Table 2 shows that in the 1970s, GDP grew by close to 5 per cent, and again, one needs, as in the case of Ayub, a thorough re-examination of the economic programme of Bhutto.

Bhutto's economic programme has been labelled a failure by his critics, and even his supporters have, under the barrage of propaganda and the changed world situation, at best been apologetic, and at worst, have joined the maligning chorus. In many ways, he was an unlucky politician and events beyond his control affected his economic programme. The economic loss of East Pakistan was strongly felt – West Pakistan 'exported' 50 per cent of its goods to the eastern wing and acquired a large amount of foreign exchange from its raw material exports. The devaluation of the Pakistani rupee by 120 per cent in May 1972 brought about significant dividends regarding export growth – in one year (1972-3), despite the loss of East Pakistan's exportable produce, West Pakistan doubled its foreign exchange earnings.

However, the 1973 OPEC price increases played havoc with Pakistan's import bill and the balance of payments deteriorated. Also, the period after 1973 saw a serious worldwide recession affecting Pakistan's exports. Recurrent domestic cotton crop failures – floods in 1973, in 1974 along with pest attacks, and worse floods in 1976 – affected Pakistan's main exports. The large nationalised units taken over by Bhutto were the most inefficient in the industrial sector, but despite this, industry experienced a reasonable growth rate, with the nationalised sector doing better than most believe.

Bhutto's government also laid the foundations for future growth and development, which his successor benefited from. Basic industries were set-up and a base for a capital goods industry was established which resulted in subsequent growth. The Middle East boom which Bhutto initiated, yet another irony in Pakistan's history, helped keep Zia in power for some years. The illiberal economic policies of Zulfiqar Ali Bhutto were responsible for growth not only in his own tenure, but also for the period after 1977.

The Second Military Government: 1977-88

General Zia's regime was more liberal in economic terms – but certainly not politically – than any of his predecessors. While the civilian-military bureaucracy did also play a prominent part in acquiring capital and in assuming the role of entrepreneur and financier, numerous individual capitalists emerged in the stable post-Bhutto era. While the trend to liberalise the economy was escalated consciously in the Zia period, the Soviet invasion of Afghanistan and the excessive involvement in Pakistan by the US also helped to speed growth. Remittances from the Middle East and aid from abroad helped launch Pakistan's second economic revolution, where the middle class emerged as a formidable economic and political category. Pakistan's growth rates in the 1980s, as Table 2 shows, were quite phenomenal. By becoming the capitalist world's 'front line' state against all things Soviet, and especially against Soviet expansionism in the region, Pakistan's government gained in terms of financial aid and resources. The impact of General Zia's martial rule, however, inflicted deep-rooted damage to Pakistani society.

Democracy and Structural Adjustment: 1988-99

The period after the death of General Zia in 1988 was marked by the return of democracy to Pakistan. Between August 1988 and October 1999, Pakistan had four general elections with Benazir Bhutto and Nawaz Sharif elected twice each. Since none of the elected governments were allowed to complete their full term, there have also been more than a few 'Caretaker' governments which have been very controversial. However, while the post-1988 period could be termed the 'Period of the Return to Democracy', we have chosen to call it the 'Era of Structural Adjustment'. Rather than the democratic process, it is a particular economic programme and process which has determined the course of Pakistan since 1988.

While the meddling of the international financial institutions, with their numerous and demanding conditionalities, resulted in the economy performing rather poorly in the 1990s, frequent changes in government did not help either. A serious debt crisis, which had been created by the profligate Zia regime in the 1980s, put additional strains on the economy and added to the already serious problems.

The Third Military Regime: 1999 Onwards

Pakistan's third coup in October 1999 was another break from the past, perhaps even a call for the end of the Zia legacy which continued into the 1990s after his death. The army's third intervention under General Musharraf ended the game of musical chairs in the political arena which had continued since 1985, in a period when democracy was searching for ground to root itself. The first two years of the Musharraf regime were largely a continuation of the 1988-99 economic policies and programmes, where growth rates took a further plunge, bringing the 1990s average to the lowest ever. However, extremely fortuitous political developments, globally and in the region, allowed General Musharraf to exploit the situation to Pakistan's advantage.

The result has been that the last fiscal year 2003-04 has achieved the highest growth rate since 1995-96, and is higher than the average for the entire decade of the '90s. As shown in a separate chapter later, with debt rescheduling and debt write-off, Pakistan's economy is set for decent growth rates. However, with nearly one-third of the population facing poverty and with the economic policies of the World Bank and IMF even more forcefully enforced, we question the claims that there has been a marked 'turnaround' in the economy; the issue of the sustainability of this growth remains highly questionable. Nevertheless, for the moment at least, General Musharraf's economic managers can rest on their laurels.

Social Development

Almost without exception, every single publication, whether by the government or by scholars and social scientists, laments the state of the social sectors in Pakistan. The high growth performance of nearly 6 per cent per annum for more than forty years is acknowledged, but at the same time, the rather dismal state of the social sectors is also highlighted. The arguments usually presented state that most governments and the public sector have ignored the social sector and have not given it enough importance or resources. Nevertheless, the more interesting question is not how the social sector has continued to remain underdeveloped, but how, with such an underdeveloped social sector, with extremely low literacy rates for example, *the economy has shown such resilient growth.* If the social sector is in as bad a state as almost all observers believe, how has the economy continued to grow at very impressive rates? Moreover, this leads to another question: can a less developed social sector continue to produce high growth, or has a time now come when growth will be highly dependent on human capital formation, as the New Growth theories suggest?

Indeed, these are interesting and important questions, the answers to which may be difficult to find. While not being able to explain how high economic growth has coexisted with very low social sector development, there is now a growing consensus that this pattern may have been one of the past, and now there is an urgent need for a highly skilled, literate, educated and healthy work force and population to deal with open trade, new technology, and the ability to maximise all human potential. This view examines the record of countries like Korea and Taiwan, and more recently of Malaysia and Thailand, and argues that without social development, economic growth and development can no longer take place. While there is growing evidence that this may be the case, one must ask whether Pakistan's elite, bureaucrats and leaders have at all learnt the lessons from the Pacific Rim and East Asian countries. Has there been any shift at all in approach, in thinking, implementation, or in finances towards the social sectors? Or is the old, tired rhetoric being repeated ad nauseam?

Some International Comparisons

It is probably not very wise to compare countries. There are too many specific factors – history, culture, governments, institutions – which may influence events and consequences in very special and specific ways. The context of each event or development must be recognised and appreciated. Often, standards of a very alien kind are imposed across a general universe, which may lead to numbers or results which are not comparable. Even so-called scientific criteria are not insensitive to their social environment, and even simply counting and comparing 'obvious facts' can be hazardous. Hence, there are numerous problems in taking a set of indicators showing the state of the health of the economy and comparing them across countries. Nevertheless, this continues to be done and there is a huge industry which churns out Ph.D.s and tomes on indicators comparing diverse nations and countries. We too, despite our criticism and concerns, follow this convention in order to indicate some salient trends.

In this section, we examine the performance of Pakistan in the social sectors in the light of that of other developing countries. While it is difficult to make comparisons across countries, it is possibly more difficult to find some countries across which comparisons can be made. In our choice of countries (see Table 3) all the eight belong to the World Bank's classification of Low Income Countries, i.e., those with a per capita GNP of less than US$ 730 based on 1993 data. This year is chosen to see how well or badly countries have performed since.

While the low income status may be the first criterion for our selection of countries, there are some others as well. India, Bangladesh and Sri Lanka share similar histories and belong to South Asia, and are also grouped together in the South Asian Association of Regional Co-operation (SAARC), and hence have some valid grounds for comparison. China is included because it is a key player in the region, used to have a GNP per capita close to that of Pakistan's, and is cited by many as a country where communist-led growth and development in the past has resulted in an egalitarian social structure with extensive social development. The new China with its liberal and open economic programme – like much of the rest of the region – is also worth observing.

Ghana and Nigeria, while very different from the Asian countries, are included because Nigeria has a large population and Ghana had a GNP per capita (in 1993) close to or equal to Pakistan's. Also, like the four South Asian countries, they have both been British colonies and hence have comparable histories. The outsider is Vietnam, which is included because it is still a Socialist state (like China), but has not had as many years of capitalism as China, and despite having a per capita GNP of only 40 per cent of Pakistan's (in 1993), has some very interesting and revealing social indicators. Possibly, GNP per capita, as is often assumed, may not be the sole, or even the key, criterion for social development. Political commitment, structure and involvement, may be equally, if not more, important.

Table 3 is not easy to interpret, indeed, if there are any interpretations which can be made from it. There are no conclusions or hard overriding truths which emerge from the table, simply observations open to conjecture.

The first row gives the GNP per capita in US dollars for 1993 for each of the eight countries, followed by the second row which shows the GNP per capita for 2003. These rates indicate the rate at which countries have grown over the last decade. China's example is significant, where in just a few years it has increased its comparative and absolute position: in 1980 China had a GNP per capita of $206 compared to Pakistan's $285, and was one of the poorest countries in the world. With a phenomenal 8.2 per cent average annual growth rate for over two decades, it has improved its position markedly. While China, Sri Lanka, Vietnam, India and even Bangladesh have all substantially improved their per capita GNP values since 1993, significantly, Pakistan, with Ghana and Nigeria, has not. Rather than be part of the dynamic growth trends of East Asia which are now also being mirrored amongst countries of South Asia, *Pakistan is now increasingly looking like a poor and underdeveloped country.*

Table 3: International Comparisons of the Social Sectors

	Pakistan	Vietnam	Bangladesh	India	Nigeria	Ghana	China	S Lanka
GNP pc 1993 $	430	170	220	300	300	430	490	600
GNP pc 2002 $	410	430	360	480	290	270	940	840
GNP pc rank 1993*	31	5	12	20	21	30	33	39
GNP pc rank 2002*	30	32	27	38	22	18	53	50
HDI rank 1993**	128	120	146	134	141	129	111	97
HDI rank 2003	144	109	139	127	152	129	104	99
Literacy rate 2001	44.0	92.7	40.6	58.0	65.4	72.7	85.8	91.9
Female literacy 2001	28.8	90.9	30.8	46.4	57.7	64.5	92.5	89.3
GDI rank 2003 +	120	89	112	103	124	104	83	80
Poverty Index rank #	65	39	72	53	54	46	26	34

Notes:* The higher the rank, the better – the poorest country is ranked 1;** The lower the rank the better – the best country is ranked 1 and the worst 175; + Best ranked 1, worst 175; # Best ranked 1, worst 74.

Source: S. Akbar Zaidi, *Issues in Pakistan's Economy* (revised and up-dated, second edition), Oxford University Press, 2004.

The GNP per capita ranking lists the position of these countries in the world on the basis of their GNP per capita. Vietnam was the fifth poorest country in the world with a GNP per capita of only $170 in 1993, and Pakistan with a GNP per capita of $430 was the 31st poorest country out of the 132 then classified by the World Bank. What is most interesting to read from this comparison of ranks of GNP per capita in 1993 and 2003, is that in line with improvements in absolute levels of GNP per capita, those countries which have done well in 1993-2003, have also done relatively better than other countries. While Vietnam was the fifth poorest in 1993, it is now the 32nd poorest, showing considerable improvement, while Pakistan joins the African countries whose ranks have worsened this decade.

While GNP per capita is a very simplistic and crude (yet indicative) measure of social development, the Human Development Index (HDI) is a larger and broader composite indicator which captures much more than just per capita income. The HDI contains three indicators: life expectancy, representing a long and healthy life; educational attainment, representing knowledge; and real GDP (in purchasing power parity dollars), representing a decent standard of living.

Thus, the HDI in Table 3 for our selected countries, unlike the GNP per capita, shows a reverse order: the higher the number, the worse the nature and extent of social development. Using the HDI, Pakistan's rank in 1993 was 128th out of 174 countries showing (a lack of) social development, but has fallen further to 144th position in 2003, mirroring the worsening trend in per capita income. In our sample, in 1993 Sri Lanka was the best of the eight countries selected (97th) and Bangladesh (146th) the worst. Ten years later Sri Lanka still remains the best at 99th position, while Nigeria has become the worst in terms of HDI ranking. Again, India, Bangladesh and Vietnam have improved their ranking, but Pakistan has fallen by as many as *fourteen positions down the HDI ladder.*

Not only is Pakistan's social and human development worsening, but so is its comparative position with regard to other countries. In terms of HDI performance, the worst 27 performers – from rank 149 to 175 – are all African countries. Of the 34 countries in the lowest HDI category called Low Human Development, only four are outside Africa. Pakistan *at position 144, happens to be one of them.* Pakistan's human and social profile looks more like that of poor African nations, rather than that of South Asian or Latin American states. Even Nepal, Bangladesh and Bhutan have better human and social development statistics than does Pakistan.

The next segment in Table 3 contains one of the most important statistics cited for social development, that of literacy. Overall adult literacy (and importantly, female literacy) is considered to be a fairly good indicator which reveals the true status of social development in any country. In New Growth theories, where human capital formation is an essential component and prerequisite for growth, literacy acts as an important proxy for many key ingredients. Also, with the need for more skills in the present electronic and computer age, with increasing stress on competition and quality, education and literacy become even more important.

Vietnam, with a GNP per capita about the same as Pakistan's, has education statistics which would put many developed high-income economies to shame, as does Sri Lanka. All the four poorest countries in our sample out-perform Pakistan very markedly. Even Bangladesh, which many in Pakistan saw as a country with few prospects, has done far better than the considerably wealthier Pakistan. Some 91 per cent of Vietnamese, and 91 per cent of Sri Lankan, women are literate, while only 29 per cent of Pakistani women can read or write. All Sri Lankan girls aged 5-9 are in school, and even Bangladesh has a very impressive record in this area, while only half of Pakistani girls are in school. Bangladesh and Pakistan are the worst performers when it comes to labour force participation by women: only 8 per cent of Bangladeshi, and 13 per cent of Pakistani women are in the labour force, compared to 47 per cent for the very poor Vietnam.

The gender-related development index (GDI), an index created by UNDP, measures the inequalities between men and women capturing differences of life expectancy, adult literacy, primary, secondary and tertiary enrolment rates, and a standard of living. The GDI in Table 3 shows that out of 175 countries, Pakistan and Nigeria perform the worst in our sample, while in Sri Lanka and China, the gender difference between men and women is less severe.

It is difficult to reach any definite conclusions from the variety of data presented in Table 3. However, some general observations can be made:

Results

1. Pakistan's economic, social and human profile over the last decade is comparable to that of African countries, rather than those of South or East Asia.

2. Most countries in our sample saw their per capita income rise in the 1993-2003 period, except for two African countries – Nigeria and Ghana – *and Pakistan*. The GDP per capita rank of these three countries has also fallen.
3. Pakistan's literacy rate is abysmally low. With the exception of Bangladesh, all countries, including Ghana and Nigeria – both of which have lower per capita incomes – have better literacy rates.
4. Pakistan's performance is better in terms of health, although with one of the highest population growth rates in the world, problems may occur in the future.
5. Almost all indicators regarding women show Pakistan as the worst performer, revealing excessive and unacceptable levels of gender discrimination.

It seems then, that despite having an impressive economic growth performance over the last many years, and outperforming other countries in the economic field, Pakistan's social development has been particularly poor. Even poorer and lesser developed countries – measured on an economic scale – have developed their social sectors well ahead of Pakistan's. From our evidence, one may surmise that economic growth, or GNP per capita, may not be the most important criterion for social development, and perhaps political will and commitment may be equally important. Pakistan's economic prosperity, especially from the earlier years upto the beginning of the 1990s, is contrasted sharply with its poor social development. Pakistan has not been able to build human capital or a skill base with which it can deal with new challenges in an increasingly global knowledge-conscious and information-oriented world.

Poverty

Towards the middle and late 1980s, there was ample evidence available which confirmed the perception that poverty had been decreasing continuously in Pakistan for almost two decades, at times quite dramatically. However, towards the very beginning of the 1990s, some concerns emerged which suggested that perhaps this decline in the poverty level had slowed down, or had even been reversed. The question raised by researchers then, in the mid-1990s, was whether poverty had returned to Pakistan, a question which was answered in the affirmative by wide recognition and consensus that poverty was on the increase, although data was still lacking to make definite and precise claims.

Later, the availability of data and interpretations and analysis of macroeconomic trends substantiated those earlier claims. Based on those trends, there is ample evidence since the end of the 1990s that poverty has continued to persist in Pakistan, and in fact, may have worsened considerably since the mid-

1980s. The question which now needs to be asked is whether poverty has become a permanent feature of Pakistan's economic and social reality, whether it is here to stay, notwithstanding attempts at poverty reduction.

Trends in Poverty

Most of the studies which estimate trends in poverty levels and poverty incidence in Pakistan use a headcount measure under an arbitrarily defined poverty line. The poverty line itself is usually based upon the concept of consumption poverty, where a minimum daily recommended calorie allowance determines the poverty line. Table 4 presents estimates of the extent of poverty in Pakistan.

The government of Pakistan acknowledges the fact that in 2004, there are at least 50 million people (32 per cent of the population) or 7.5 million households that fall below the poverty line. Table 4 confirms the view that poverty first rose in the 1960s, after which it has seen a continuous decline until around 1987-88, after which, for the most part, there has been another rise in the incidence of poverty in the country. Almost all the recent literature on poverty in Pakistan seems to suggest that there is a growing consensus that poverty has increased since the early, and most certainly, the mid-1990s. Moreover, despite different measurements and estimates, there is almost complete agreement that there was a formidable decline in poverty in the period 1969-70 to 1979, a drop of almost 16 percentage points over the decade, and an equally impressive fall of 13 percentage points in the next decade, until 1987-88. Moreover, in the 1980s, the period 1984-85 to 1987-88 shows a drop in poverty by more than 7 percentage points.[1]

Another noticeable trend from Table 4 is the more or less consistent fall in *urban* poverty throughout the last forty-six years. Although only 23 percent of the population lived in cities in the early 1960s compared to more than forty percent today, this decline in urban poverty has continued even when there was a rise in rural (hence, overall) poverty. However, the dramatic fall in poverty in the 1970s was attributed to the huge reduction in rural poverty which accounted for a much larger proportion of the population and of the poor.

If we examine trends in income distribution, we observe that during the 1960s when there was high growth and poverty increased, the Gini coefficient fell from 0.355 to 0.33, improving the distribution of income for both urban and rural areas (see Table 5).[2] In the 1970s, there was again

---

1. It is important to state that due to changes in definition and measurement, one cannot strictly compare figures on poverty from the past with current statistics since most studies have used different sets of criteria to capture the level and extent of poverty. What is more important, however, is not the exact number or proportion of those below the poverty line, but the trend and direction. While there is some debate on exact numbers, there is complete agreement that the trend of poverty has worsened.
2. The Gini coefficient is a measure which shows the degree of income inequality over time and/or across countries. The closer the Gini is to 1.00, the greater the inequality, and the closer it is to 0.00, the more equitable the income distribution.

an inverse relationship between poverty and income distribution, with the latter improving and the former worsening. Both the 1980s and the 1990s saw poverty and income distribution moving in the same direction, with poverty falling in the 1980s and income distribution improving; the decade of the 1990s had the opposite trends. Currently, income distribution based on the Gini coefficient is worse than what it was in the early 1960s. Moreover, concentration of income has also worsened in recent years, with the income share of the highest twenty percent of the population increasing over time, and that of the lowest twenty percent falling.

Table 4: Trends in Poverty: Proportion of Poor (Headcount %)

Year	Total	Rural	Urban
1963-64	40.24	38.94	44.53
1966-67	44.50	45.62	40.96
1969-70	46.53	49.11	38.76
1979	30.68	32.51	25.94
1984-85	24.47	25.87	21.17
1987-88	17.32	18.32	14.99
1992-93	22.40	23.35	15.50
1996-97	31.00	32.00	27.00
1998-99	32.60	34.80	25.90

Source: Government of Pakistan, *Pakistan Economic Survey,* various issues, Islamabad.

Table 5: Trends in the Gini Coefficient

Year	Total	Rural	Urban
1963-64	0.355	0.348	0.368
1969-70	0.330	0.295	0.361
1971-72	0.344	0.309	0.381
1979	0.375	0.319	0.380
1984-85	0.428	0.345	0.379
1985-86	0.355	0.330	0.354
1990-91	0.407	0.410	0.390
1998-99	0.410	0.40	0.33

Source: Government of Pakistan, *Pakistan Economic Survey*, various issues, Islamabad.

Figure 1: Poverty Trends

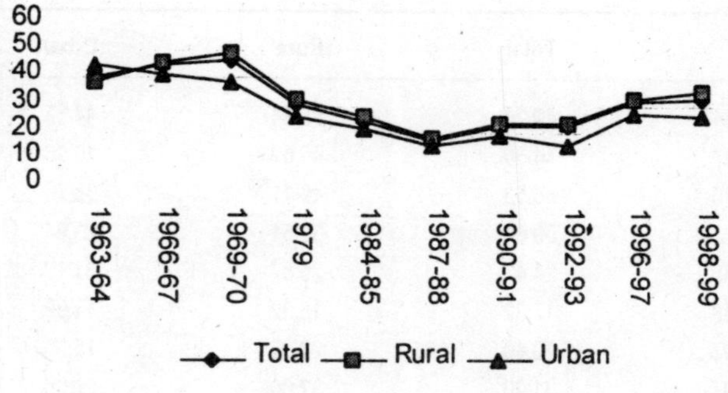

Figure 2: Trends in Income Inequality

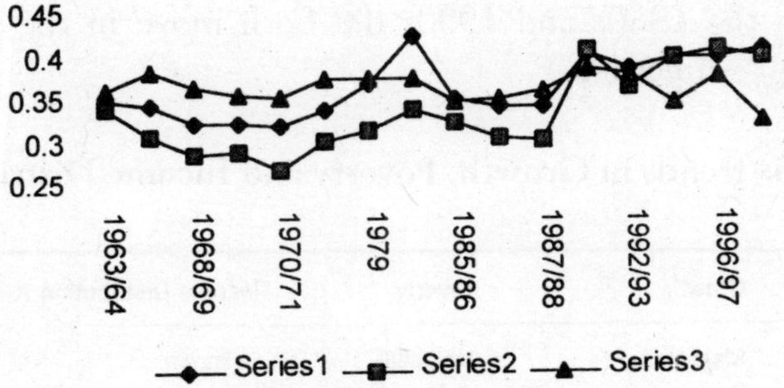

Explaining the Trends in Poverty

In much of the literature that has examined poverty trends in Pakistan, a key concern has been the relationship between economic growth and poverty. Although most authors have argued and cautioned that there are no hard and fast rules which reveal an automatic and strong correlation, poverty is seen to be closely linked to, if not determined by, economic growth. In fact, *economic growth is considered to be an essential prerequisite for poverty reduction.* Almost every study examining the relationship of economic growth with poverty alleviation has argued that economic growth is the foundation on which poverty reduction can be achieved, and that economic growth plays a dominant role in poverty alleviation; without strong and sustained economic growth, poverty alleviation is not possible. A broad trend in the incidence of poverty can be gauged from Table 6, where trends in economic growth and poverty are presented over the last five decades. The table suggests, perhaps, that for the 1960s and 1970s, growth and poverty did not seem to have the 'correct' relationship, and only in the 1980s and 1990s did both move in the right – inverse – direction.

Table 6: Trends in Growth, Poverty and Income Distribution

Decade	Growth	Poverty	Income Distribution (Gini)
1950s	Stagnated	Persisted	Unknown
1960s	Rapid Increase	Increased	Improved
1970s	Slow, Stagnated	Declined	Worsened
1980s	Rapid Increase	Declined	Rapid deterioration, followed by rapid improvement
1990s	Substantial Decline	Increased Considerably	Worsened

Every single indicator which has some poverty reducing impact, such as economic growth, manufacturing sector growth, employment, public expenditure, development expenditure, remittances and subsidies, has worsened over the last decade. The impact on poverty should be equally clear. It is no surprise then, that poverty has increased in Pakistan over the last decade and, given the current macro-economic trends, is likely to persist and possibly increase over the next few years.

Structural Reforms and the Impact of Globalisation

Pakistan has been liberalising and opening up its economy for many years now, especially since 1988 when it undertook the first of many structural adjustment programmes, under the guise of different IMF facilities. Currently, it is working under a $1.3 billion Poverty Reduction and Growth Fund facility, under which the process of privatisation and liberalisation has continued.

The main features of the reforms – which have continued despite changes in governments – has been a reduction in the fiscal deficit, privatisation of state industries, utility rationalisation, trade reforms, financial sector reforms, and a host of other interventions. The fiscal deficit has been a core indicator which has had an impact on numerous other sectors. Because of Pakistan's accumulated debt and the interest payments which have to be paid each year, the role of the government's budget deficit has been central. In the 1980s, the fiscal deficit used to be around 7 or 8 percent each year – the 1980s average was 7.1 percent of the GDP and 6.9 percent for the 1990s – and has been brought down to around 4.6 percent in 2002-03. The government is working towards a target of 4 percent of GDP.

This fiscal deficit has been reduced by cutting government expenditure – sadly, largely development expenditure – increasing the tax base by including more individuals in the tax net and by expanding the scope of taxation, largely by imposing a General Sales Tax. Some restructuring of the Central Board of Revenue has also been undertaken as part of the tax reforms. Loss-making public sector corporations have either been closed down or privatised.

Over seventy units in ten years have been privatised including four very large public sector banks. The government has an ambitious agenda of privatising some large public sector utilities also in the oil and gas, electricity generation and transmission sectors. To cut the fiscal deficit further, subsidies to agriculture and on fertilisers have also been reduced. Moreover, there are no restrictions on investment of almost any kind. Governments have made it very easy for foreign investors to invest in Pakistan and to remit profits. In fact, some of the large companies which have been privatised have been sold to foreign investors.

Trade reforms have largely meant a reduction in customs tariffs, from a high maximum tariff rate of 225 percent in 1990, to 25 percent today, with the number of tariff slabs reduced to 4. This has been done to make Pakistan's industry more competitive and exposed to foreign competition in preparation for WTO's requirements in 2005. Numerous restrictions on the import or export of commodities have been removed, allowing a freer trade regime.

Pakistan's Textiles in a Globalised World

Since textiles and garments constitute a large share of Pakistan's exports – 67 percent of all exports in 2002-03 – in this section we examine the impact of globalisation and the WTO on these commodities. Pakistan is the world's fourth largest cotton producer with annual production around 10-11 million bales and its cotton fibre is considered to be one of the best in the world, but due to poor picking, ginning and elimination of contamination, it loses this advantage. Pakistan is also ranked fourth in terms of spindles and twelfth in terms of rotors installed. Pakistan is the world's fourth largest cotton yarn producer as well after China, India and the USA.

About 70 percent of Pakistan's yarn production is coarse cotton yarn and only 3 percent is of fine and super fine counts. Pakistan is one of the largest exporters of cotton yarn in the world, in terms of quantity, but in terms of value it captures only 5 per cent of the export market. This suggests the low value added nature of Pakistan's exports of yarn.

In terms of weaving as well, Pakistan is the world's fourth largest exporter of woven cloth, although much of the woven fabric is of low value, which is attributed to the low level of technology both in the weaving and processing sector, with processing being the weakest link in the entire textile value chain. In the world's largest market of cotton fabrics, Pakistan's finished cloth share is extremely small, only 3 per cent of global trade. Pakistan occupies a dominant position in the low cost and low quality cotton fabrics market.

The reason for this is that apart from a small number, the majority of the processing units in Pakistan are not integrated but independent commercial dyeing, printing and finishing units. Most of these units have low dyeing technology catering to the processing requirements of the low-end knitting and woven fabric manufacturers. Textile made-ups (towels and bed-sheets) as well as the garment industry's demand is also met by such units.

Textile processing is a technology-oriented business which requires capital-intensive technology, but most of Pakistan's machinery in this sector is more than fifteen years old and requires a major overhaul to upgrade it to meet high quality and modern standards. The tendency is to invest in the printing side of the industry even though the dyed fabric is a higher value product compared to printed fabric and fetches a higher price. This trend is driven by the dominance of the power loom sector for the supply of woven fabrics. There is a need to invest in the dyeing side of the industry rather than printing which will result in the higher unit price of the fabric being exported.

In the textile sector, the biggest growth is taking place in the share of clothing and apparel. Since the 1990s, the clothing trade has grown at a rate of 82 per cent compared to textiles (4 percent), with both accounting for around $160 billion of this market worldwide. Pakistan has at best a 1 percent share of the global apparel market, primarily because Pakistan's exports have a low share of the value added goods market, which continues to increase. This means that since Pakistan has a higher share in the low value added segment of the market, its export earnings will remain low unless the textile industry diversifies and moves into the high value added, quality garments and made-ups sector.

Pakistan, like all countries of the world, is in the process of implementing the provisions of the World Trade Organisation's guidelines and agreements. Trade and industrial sectors have been undergoing radical change in compliance, first with the structural adjustment programmes of the IMF and World Bank, and more recently, in compliance with GATT and WTO rules and regulations, which are to come into force and be fully effective (the September 2003 failure of the Cancun Round of negotiations notwithstanding) by January 2005. These rules provide the legal framework for international commerce and there are various protocols which affect different sectors.

Countries are required to improve access to foreign goods and markets by reducing/eliminating tariffs and abolishing quotas. In addition, subsidies both on exports, credit and on domestic goods are to be eliminated and countervailing and anti-dumping measures taken. Let us see how these measures will affect Pakistan's textiles, which constitute more than sixty per cent of Pakistan's exports.

The international trade in textiles and clothing has been subject to quantitative restrictions in industrial countries. Historically, these restrictions were governed by the Multi-Fibre Agreement (MFA) which started in 1974 and was last extended up to 31 December, 1994. Following the Uruguay Round of multilateral trade negotiations (1986-1994), the WTO Agreement on Textiles and Clothing (ATC) came into force from 1 January 1995. It envisaged a transitional period of ten years till 31 December 2004 by when the MFA restrictions on textiles and clothing would be removed in four phases. So far, three of these phases have been implemented and the last phase is in process.

From 1 January 2005, the entire textiles and clothing sector will be integrated with GATT 1994 and there will cease to be any restrictions on imports of textiles by any of the WTO members. The ATC principle removes all quantitative restrictions by industrial countries on imports of textiles and clothing from all countries, bringing in a new, forceful era of global competition. The new regime will have a significant impact on countries which were enjoying secured market access which they will no longer have. On the other hand, countries which were being constrained by quotas will now be able to enhance market access under the new, 'free' regime.

Before we see how this will have an impact on Pakistan, let us briefly look at what the old regime of restrictions and reforms was like. First of all, the incidence of protection on textile and clothing in industrialised countries has been much higher than on other manufactured products. On an average, these tariffs were three or four times more than those on other manufactured products, with tariffs increasing with each stage of processing.[1] Average tariffs on fibres were

1. Din, Musleh-ud and Kalbe Abbas, 'The Uruguay Round and Agreement and Pakistan's Trade in Textiles and Clothing', Paper presented at the 15th Annual General Meeting and Conference, Pakistan Society of Development Economists, November 1999.

about 1 per cent, while on clothing they were often more than 20 per cent.

Musleh-ud-Din and Kalbe Abbas present a very interesting analysis of what the earlier MFA tariff and quantitative regime was doing. They argue that the MFA has restricted potential imports into major industrial markets and that growth in the volume of textiles and clothing exports of developing countries has been lower because of the agreement. They make numerous important points and say: 'Countries that are efficient producers of textiles and clothing products have been particularly vulnerable to the imposition or tightening of MFA quotas ... Other effects of the MFA include trade diversion to less restricted countries away from competitive suppliers ... The rigidities of the quota system under the MFA have also enabled traditional suppliers to maintain their market shares despite declining competitiveness, and thus have prevented more efficient new entrants from competing on equal terms.'[2]

The Pakistan government is expected to loosen its controls on cotton exports under WTO commitments. The All Pakistan Textile Manufacturers Association (APTMA) argues that the unrestricted export of cotton would deprive the spinning industry of raw material and push up production costs to uneconomic levels. Since all countries are to remove trade barriers (i.e., import restrictions) and as quotas are to be removed from other garment and made-up producing countries as well, there is likely to be a greater demand for Pakistani

2. Ibid., p. 7.

yarn and fabric and, therefore, there will be even less cotton available for local producers.

According to WTO rules, the government will not be in a position to intervene either in terms of discouraging exports of cotton, yarn or fabrics, or to provide subsidies to garments and made-up exporters. Textile manufacturers fear that their industry will suffer and Pakistan will lose out on valuable exports. However, it is possible that farmers, or at least owners of large pieces of land on which cotton is grown, will benefit by access to the free market.

One argument put forward by many Pakistani policy makers and industrialists, is that after 2005, when a quota-free world takes over, Pakistan's main exports, textiles, will receive a huge boost. The exports will increase because they will no longer be restricted by quotas, as they are at present. On the face of it, this makes a lot of sense. After all, as the argument goes, developed countries can buy only a certain amount of Pakistan's textiles constrained by set quotas. In addition, there are those in Pakistan who argue that quotas in Pakistan were being sold at a premium in the black market since there was perceived to be a shortage of quotas, and this premium was borne as an additional cost by textile exporters and in some cases was considered to constitute a major part of the exported item's price. Both these factors suggest that Pakistan's textile exports will increase as one element of cost will be reduced and there will be a greater demand. But, this is only one side of the picture.

First of all, Pakistan will not be the only country which will have no quota restrictions – all countries, including

Pakistan's main competitors like China, India and Turkey, will be able to sell as much as they possibly can. In fact one argument in the past has been that Pakistan should be grateful for the existence of a quota regime because it limits imports from competitors like China and India and allows at least some Pakistani textiles to get through. A quota-free regime means increased competition and only the best and cheapest products will sell. There is no guarantee that Pakistan will meet the new standards and one cannot say for sure that exports will increase; they may even fall.

While tariff and quantity restrictions will be done away with under the WTO regime, new forms of non-tariff barriers will be imposed. Sanitary and environmental standards can be imposed, as they were some years ago in the case of Pakistan's surgical goods exports. Social barriers, or those pertaining to child labour or other kinds of restrictions can circumvent the no-barriers provision. Political, rather than economic or trade-related, factors may come to dominate the new, free trade world order.

In the light of globalisation and WTO agreements, Pakistan's textile sector is likely to enter a completely different realm of competition and issues. Musleh-ud-Din and Kalbe Abbas[3] have examined the impact of these changes and in the light of these new conditions, have made some recommendations

---

3. Din, Musleh-ud and Kalbe Abbas, 'The Uruguay Round and Agreement and Pakistan's Trade in Textiles and Clothing', Paper presented at the 15th Annual General Meeting and Conference, Pakistan Society of Development Economists, November 1999.

which are worth considering. They argue that in the past although the textile and clothing industry has been protected under high tariffs, with subsidies, concessionary finances, subsidised cotton prices and numerous other incentives and breaks, it has not been able to achieve a high level of efficiency, nor has it been able to enter the high end of the quality market.

In order to take advantage of the changes, Pakistan will have to improve its quality standards across the board, right from raw cotton to finished products. More research is required in the development of different types of cotton, especially the long-staple superior varieties. Musleh-ud-Din and Kalbe Abbas also recommend that Pakistan must move into synthetic fibres as this sector has been growing in recent years. Most importantly, Pakistan will have to move into higher value added products rather than concentrate on low-end or intermediate products. As stated earlier, this would require a strong and modern weaving and processing base. Better management, design and efficiency are also required to deal with the new environment after 2005.

Pakistan in South Asia

India and Pakistan: A Brief Comparison

In 1990, both Pakistan and India had identical per capita incomes, at $390 each. In 2001, for which the latest figures are available, Pakistan's per capita income was $420, and India's $ 460 (see Table 7). It is probable, given Pakistan's economic performance compared to India's in the last three years, that the difference has widened further. What is more suggestive, and worrying for Pakistan, is the comparison between India and Pakistan in terms of per capita income when we use a far more useful measure called the Purchasing Power Parity (PPP) figures. These PPP comparisons enable a far better assessment of the standard of living in terms of what people can actually purchase, after taking into account differences in prices. Pakistan's per capita PPP income in 1990 was $1360, while India's was $1380. In 2001, Pakistan's per capita PPP had risen to $1860, a growth of $500 or 37 percent. Meanwhile, India's PPP per capita in this decade had *more than doubled*, having risen to $2820 per capita. Indeed, a highly impressive achievement.

Table 7: India-Pakistan: A Comparison

	Population (in Millions)		GNI per capita ($)		GNI per capita at PPP ($)	
	1990	2001	1990	2001	1990	2001
India	850	1032	390	460	1380	2820
Pakistan	105	141	390	420	1360	1860

Source: Chadha, Rajesh and Devender Pratap, 'New Era of India-Pakistan Trade Relations: More Butter and Less Guns', unpublished mimeograph, New Delhi: 2003.

This critical indicator, that of per capita income, is only the first of numerous social and economic indicators which show the growing difference between India and Pakistan during the 1990s, a trend which has increased further in these last three years, and is going to keep rising for a considerable time to come into the future. With India set to achieve a GDP growth rate of 8 percent in 2003-04 and with a trend rate of above 6 percent likely to persist for some years to come, even the exceptional 5.1 percent GDP growth for Pakistan in 2002-03 and the 6.4 percent in 2003-04 will cause the gap to increase further. Some additional figures will support this claim.

What is particularly interesting is that in the decade 1980-90, Pakistan's economic performance measured in terms of growth rates in agriculture, industry, merchandise exports, and even GDP, was better than that of India. In the 1990s, however, following both Pakistan and India's economic reforms and liberalisation – implemented very differently, no doubt – India's growth rates for the decade in all these sectors (except agriculture) were not just higher, but significantly higher (often twice as high) in every single category (see Table 8). Perhaps the most extraordinary difference in comparative growth trends between India and Pakistan is in India's more than double export growth, and the four-times higher growth in new investment measured by Gross Capital Formation. Pakistan has had very little addition to capital in the 1990s, a trend which, sadly, has worsened in the last two years following 9/11 and Pakistan's role in the war against terror.

Table 8: Economic Structure and Trade Dependence of India and Pakistan

Country/ Share	Sectoral Value added as % of GDP									Ratio Trade/GDP		
	Agriculture			Industry			Services					
	1980	1990	2000	1980	1990	2000	1980	1990	2000	1980	1990	2000
India	39	31	25	24	28	27	37	41	48	16	17	31
Pakistan	30	26	26	25	25	23	46	49	51	37	39	35

Note: Trade is the sum of exports and imports of Good and Services.

Source: Chadha, Rajesh and Devender Pratap, 'New Era of India-Pakistan Trade Relations: More Butter and Less Guns', unpublished mimeograph, New Delhi, 2003.

Table 9: Growth of Sectoral GDP, Merchandise Export and Gross Capital Formation in India and Pakistan

Average Annual Growth (%)												
Country	Agriculture		Industry		Services		GDP		Merchandise Exports		Gross Capital Formation	
	1980-90	1990-2000	1980-90	1990-2000	1980-90	1990-2000	1980-90	1990-2000	1980-90	1990-2000	1980-90	1990-2000
India	3.1	3	6.9	6.4	7.0	8.0	5.8	6	7.3	9.5	6.6	7.9
Pakistan	4.3	4.4	7.3	3.9	6.8	4.4	6.3	3.7	8.1	4.3	5.8	1.8

Source: Chadha, Rajesh and Devender Pratap, 'New Era of India-Pakistan Trade Relations: More Butter and Less Guns', unpublished mimeograph, New Delhi, 2003.

Since 1993, India's growth rate has been higher than Pakistan's *in every single year*, and in four years of the last ten, India's growth rate has been *double Pakistan's*. This is not all. If we look at all the seven SAARC countries, today even Bangladesh and Nepal perform far better than Pakistan, and this is especially apparent if we compare current growth rates with those of the 1980s. In the 1980s, Pakistan had the second highest GDP growth rate after the Maldives. In the 1990s, Pakistan's GDP growth rate was the lowest of the seven.

It is not just these 'hard' economic statistics which show how Pakistan has been left behind by other SAARC countries and particularly by India, but numerous other softer indicators also re-emphasise this trend. The UN Human Development Index (HDI) is a good indicator of broad social development in a country and includes social indicators as well as economic ones. In the HDI ranking of 1991, Pakistan was placed higher (better) than India and Bangladesh. In 2003, India is ranked far higher than Pakistan, as is Bangladesh. More importantly,

Pakistan's rank fell from being 138th to 144th in just one year, 2002-03, and Nepal and Pakistan are the only two non-African countries to be classified in the low human development group. Clearly, a most ignoble achievement.

There are numerous other social and economic indicators which highlight the fact that Pakistan has been left far behind. Poverty in India, for example, has fallen from 45 percent of the population in 1983 to 26 percent today. In Pakistan it increased from 17 percent in 1987 to 32 percent today. Not only do the past trends show a worsening gap, but while Pakistan was celebrating a 6.4 percent growth in GDP for the first time since 1995, hoping to achieve the same rate this year, the Reserve Bank of India was increasing its earlier expectations to well above six percent for the next three years for India with a growth of over 8 percent in 2003-04.

The difference is clear: India's economic growth has by far overtaken Pakistan's, a trend which is unlikely to be reversed for some time to come.

Pakistan's Trade With India[1]

Pakistan and India have been trading with each other since 1947, and in the last 57 years, trade has come to a complete halt or been suspended for only nine years, between 1965-74.

---

1. This part of this monograph is drawn from my earlier paper: Zaidi, S. Akbar 'Pakistan's Development Options: Does India Matter At All?' This paper was presented at the *Deterrence Theory and South Asia Workshop*, UPIAS, New Delhi, August 26-27, 2003. For an earlier assessment of this theme also see: Sridharan, E., 'Economic Cooperation and Security Spill-Overs: The Case of India and Pakistan', in Krepon, Michael and Chris Gagne (editors), *Economic Confidence-Building and Regional Security*, The Henry L. Stimson Centre, Report No 36,

However, despite a largely uninterrupted trade regime since 1974, the extent of trade between India and Pakistan is limited and almost negligible, as Table 10 shows. Chadha and Pratap, using figures only for legal trade, state:

> While about 4.5 per cent of India's total exports are directed to South Asia, the figure is 3 per cent in the case of Pakistan.[2] Exports to Pakistan constitute about 8 per cent of India's total exports to South Asia. Pakistan's exports to India have a higher average share of about 40 per cent, during 1998-2000, of Pakistan's total exports to South Asia compared with an average share of about 17 per cent during 1995-1997. In the case of imports, 0.8 per cent of India's imports originate from South Asia and the figure is 0.5 per cent for Pakistan. Within India's imports from South Asia, 36 per cent originate from Pakistan. Pakistan sources 69 per cent of its total imports from South Asia from India. Clearly, India and Pakistan are two major trading partners among the South Asian countries despite of all hurdles.[3]

---

and Security Spill-Overs: The Case of India and Pakistan', in Krepon, Michael and Chris Gagne (editors), *Economic Confidence-Building and Regional Security*, The Henry L. Stimson Centre, Report No 36, Washington, October 2000; Zaidi, S. Akbar, 'Economic Confidence Building Measures in South Asia: Trade as a Precursor to Peace with India', in Ahmar, Moonis (ed.), *The Challenge of Confidence Building in South Asia*, Haranand Publications, New Delhi, 2001; and Chadha, Rajesh and Devender Pratap, 'New Era of India-Pakistan Trade Relations: More Butter and Less Guns', unpublished mimeograph, New Delhi, 2003.

2. Average for three years, viz. 1998-2000.
3. Chadha and Pratap, op. cit., p. 56 (footnote 1).

There are some curious facts about trade between India and Pakistan which need to be highlighted and Tables 10-13 do this. Firstly, open, formal (legal) trade between the two countries is very small, and in the last decade has varied between a low of $106 million in 1994-95 which was a mere 0.6 percent of Pakistan's total trade that year, to a high of $321 million in 1998-99 or 1.9 percent of Pakistan's total trade. Clearly the volume and scale of trade between the two countries is very small in absolute terms and as part of the total trade of both countries. However, given the political history of the two countries with many wars and consistently poor diplomatic relations affecting trade and economic co-operation, it is believed that third-country trade and smuggling increase the volume of trade from anywhere between $1–1.5 billion, still a small number, but of somewhat more significance, particularly for the smaller economy of Pakistan.

Table 10: India-Pakistan Trade 1990-2000 (max and min range, in percent)

Share of India's total Exports, 1990-2000:	to South Asia: 2.7-5.1
	to Pakistan: 0.2-0.4
Share of India's total Imports, 1990-2000:	from South Asia: 0.4-0.8
	from Pakistan: 0.2-0.6
Share of Pakistan's total Exports, 1990-2000:	to South Asia: 2.6-4.9
	to India: 0.4-2.4
Share of Pakistan's total Imports, 1990-2000:	from South Asia: 0.4-1.7
	from India: 0.2-0.6

Source: Chadha, Rajesh and Devender Pratap, 'New Era of India-Pakistan Trade Relations: More Butter and Less Guns', unpublished mimeograph, New Delhi, 2003.

Table 11: Pakistan's Total Trade and Trade with India 1992-2002 (in million dollars)

	1992-93	1993-94	1994-95	1995-96	1996-97	1997-98	1998-99	1999-2000	2000-01	2001-02
Total										
Exprt	6819	6812	8141	8707	8323	8627	7779	8568	9201	9134
Imprt	9963	8561	10401	11804	11894	10118	9431	10309	10728	10339
India										
Exprt	83	42	42	41	36	89	175	54	55	49
Imprt	67	70	64	95	197	153	146	127	235	187

Source: State Bank of Pakistan, *Annual Report*, various years, Karachi.

Although much is made of the rather limited volume of trade between India and Pakistan, a number of points, especially from the Pakistani angle, have been overlooked. Firstly, the quantum of official trade between the two countries of between two to three hundred million dollars, is supplemented with illicit trade between the two countries, and the trade of goods which originate in either country but are imported through a third country. This recalculation increases the total trade between the countries by a factor of four or five. This is a significant increase, especially when one considers the fact that already, for Pakistan at least, using the official bilateral trade figures alone, India is the main trading partner in the SAARC region. The new set of figures would further enhance that dominance. Compared to trade with its neighbours Afghanistan, Iran and China, Pakistan's trade with India is far greater than with the former two, and with the new set of figures, India comes a close second to China. Clearly, despite an unfavourable trade, economic and political environment, there is already substantial trade between Pakistan and India which has even greater economic possibilities.

Perhaps the most curious fact about Pakistan's trade with India is this assumption that it is so low. Certainly official figures, as we show in Table 10, do enforce that perception, but even if we limit ourselves to these official figures, some rather interesting observations emerge. For example, in recent years when imports from India have ranged from $145 million in 1998-99 to $235 million in 2000-01 and to $187 million in 2001-02 (the latest complete figures), *India emerges as Pakistan's 16*th *biggest trading partner in terms of imports*. This figure is even more interesting since the four largest importers into Pakistan are oil-exporting countries (Saudi Arabia, UAE and Kuwait) and Malaysia which exports mainly palm oil to Pakistan. Despite hostilities, wars and diplomatic breakdowns, Pakistan imports (based only on official figures, one must emphasise, which are perhaps a third of actual volume) more from India than it does from France, Canada, Switzerland, the Netherlands, Turkey, Iran or even Thailand! Indeed, a most amazing state given the political relations between the two countries. In terms of total trade, exports and imports based on the under-reported 'official' trade between the two countries, India ranks 21st as Pakistan's trading partner. Clearly, the possibilities of gains from opening trade are tremendous, especially if we look at the nature of trade between the two countries.

In the decade 1990-2000, Pakistan has had a trade surplus with India in only three of these ten years, importing far more than it exports. Most of Pakistan's exports to India have been in the 'food and related' category, rather than in raw materials, manufactured goods or intermediate products. India's exports to Pakistan have been distributed over the categories 'agricultural and allied products', manufactured goods and chemical and chemical related products[4] (see tables 12 and 13). Pakistan and India's imports have both been heavily influenced by single commodity – usually food – items as the tables show, although Pakistan also does import chemicals and tyre related products. Moreover, the tables also show considerable inconsistency and annual variability between the types of commodities imported by both countries; other than food items, there is little consistency in the pattern of traded commodities. Perhaps this suggests a curious fact, that both countries, despite extremely poor political and diplomatic relations, do turn to each other in times of need.

Table 12: Pakistan's Imports from India: 2000-02 (thousands of rupees)

	2001-02	2000-01
Total Imports	Rs 11,471,155	Rs 13,928,480
	%	%
Agriculture and Food	16	53
(Sugar)	(10)	(39)
Iron and manganese ore	9	6
Chemicals	38	21
(Pure Xylenes)	(17)	(1)
Medicinal inputs	4	2
Plastics	8	4
Tyres and Rubber	7	4

Note: Agriculture and food includes 'residue of soyabeans oil-cake', and Chemicals includes dyes, paint and ink.

Source: Federal Bureau of Statistics, *Annual Trade Statistics 2001-02*, Government of Pakistan, Islamabad, 2003.

4. Sridharan, E., op. cit., p. 55-56 (footnote 1).

Table 13: Pakistan's Exports to India 2000-02 (in thousands of rupees)

	2001-02	2000-01
Total Exports	Rs 3,246,436	Rs 2,777,405
	%	%
Agriculture and Food	66	66
(Dates)	(42)	(35)
(Rice)		(23)
Asafoetida	5	-
Crude Petroleum	-	8
Cotton staple	-	10
Cotton yarn and related	18	5
(Cotton tents)	(12)	(-)

Source: Federal Bureau of Statistics, *Annual Trade Statistics 2001-02*, Government of Pakistan, Islamabad, 2003.

It is also worth highlighting some observations which give India-Pakistan trade a rather ironic twist. It was in 1977-78, when Pakistan was under General Zia ul Haq's martial law, that trade between the two countries received an impetus, following the 1974 Protocol for the restoration of commercial relations on a government to government basis, signed by the two countries after the 1971 war. Again, still under a military government in 1987, Pakistan increased the number of permitted traded goods with India nearly six-fold, from 42 to 249, a measure which led to a three-fold increase in the following three years.[5] Also, although both countries avoid improving their mutual trading status, both turn to each other

5. Government of Pakistan, op. cit., p. 16.

during crises and shortfalls of edible products. In 1990, India helped Pakistan tide over an onion and potato crisis, and again Pakistan imported 50,000 tons of sugar from India on an emergency basis in 1997. Likewise, India has also depended on Pakistan for sugar, potatoes, onions and chillies, at the time of a shortage.

Most interesting is the fact that the largest volume of trade between the two countries *ever*, was in Pakistan's fiscal year 1998-99, when it was valued at $320 million. Pakistan's fiscal year runs from July to June, which means that this was the fiscal year which followed the May 1998 nuclear tests by both countries, included the Lahore Declaration of February 1999, as well as the Kargil war of May and June 1999. By any measure, this was a rather eventful year in South Asia, and yet, registered the largest volume of trade. Moreover, in 2000-01, in General Musharraf's first full year as the Chief Executive/President, imports from India were $235 million, *the highest ever*. This suggests two things: India and Pakistan, despite huge differences, trade with each other at times of shortfalls and crises, and, even a military ruler can improve (trade) relations with India if need be.

E. Sridharan argues that 'India does not import any of Pakistan's major exports. Nor does Pakistan import any of India's major exports'[6] – as we show in the earlier tables. He explains this fact in terms of trade-related and economic (rather than political) arguments, and says that this is because of the competitive rather than complementary nature of the

6. Sridharan, op. cit., p. 55-56 (footnote 1).

two economies exporting similar products, and argues that there is the 'general tendency for poor countries to trade with developed ones rather than with their neighbours until a certain level of development has been achieved'.[7] This explains the reasons why trade did not take place between the two countries, and he thinks that 'the real scope for trade and investment is in the future and begins now'.[8] For Sridharan, however, rather than the trade of goods and commodities, 'the real potential for economic co-operation today is in energy, for example, a gas pipeline and the export of electricity ...'.[9] Not denying the fact that past and existing patterns of trade between the two neighbours have been rather limited, we still see far greater opportunities than does Sridharan.

This point of view is also propagated by the Ministry of Commerce of the Government of Pakistan, which conducted an extensive study on the prospects and implications of trade with India. The study published by the Ministry had, as a part of its team, a number of very prominent businessmen, and they all advocated increased and fair trade with India. It is worth looking at some of the ideas which form this Report.

The Ministry of Commerce study argues that there are numerous advantages to trade between neighbours, as there are low transportation costs, cultural similarities which influence taste and cause profitable complementarities to emerge. In addition, transaction costs are also lowered and such trade

---

7. Ibid., p. 70.
8. Ibid., p. 89.
9. Ibid., p. 89.

'facilitates the flow of ideas and knowledge that strengthen international competitiveness'.[10] The study looks at a number of sectors in the Pakistan economy and concludes that *'the economic benefits of liberalizing trade with India outweigh costs'*.[11] Consumers in Pakistan will benefit 'unambiguously' because of lower prices, and the government will get far greater revenue from legalising the existing illicit border trade. Moreover, 'important segments of producers would also benefit because of increased competitiveness and market access to a much larger Indian economy'.[12]

A study by the Karachi Chamber of Commerce and Industry also endorses the idea of trade with India, on the grounds that now having signed the agreements which have led to the setting up of the World Trade Organisation, all signatory members have to be treated equally, and understands that giving the Most Favoured Nation status to India: 'is not a special favour to India, but an obligation under WTO and an economic and geopolitical imperative'.[13] In this new world order, the study argues, Pakistan has to face competition from all countries including India, and hence 'instead of shying away, we should be well prepared to face the eventuality. In any case, salvation lies in streamlining of

10. Government of Pakistan, Ministry of Commerce, *Pakistan-India Trade: Transition to the GATT Regime*, Islamabad, September 1996, p. 1.
11. Ibid., p. 2, emphasis added.
12. Ibid., p. 2.
13. Karachi Chamber of Commerce and Industry (KCCI), *Freer Trade With India: Its Raison d'être and Impact*, Research and Development Cell, KCCI, Karachi, March 1996, p. 1.

operations and upgrading of technology which was long overdue.'[14]

This study does present a sector-wise analysis of trade with India and shows the impact on each sector, looking at numerous aspects including what it calls 'silver linings'. For example, it feels that while the opening up of trade with India is likely to affect the engineering sector, cheaper steel and iron ore imports from India will have a positive overall impact and 'will result in the reduction of very high inventory costs of the engineering sector'.[15] However, the main argument which this Report seems to be making, is that *Pakistan trades with almost every country in the world, so why not with India?*

There is also the important issue of globalisation and its impact. All the countries of the world are affected by it, some favourably and others not so favourably. To take further advantage or to protect themselves from the negative impact of globalisation, many neighbouring countries have established trading blocs and currently around 60 percent of world trade takes place through regional trading arrangements. There are huge advantages and benefits to such regional trading arrangements, yet, 'South Asia is the only major world region not to move towards regional co-operation and integration'.[16] Clearly, normalisation of trading ties between India and Pakistan should be seen as a first step to such trading arrangements. As Burki argues, 'our policy-makers must be cognisant of the

---

14. Ibid., p. 3.
15. Ibid., p. 5.
16. Burki, Shahid Javed, 'The Themes to be Explored', *DAWN*, Karachi, January 23, 2001.

fact that the world is organising itself into a number of regional arrangements and we in Pakistan cannot afford to be left out of them'.[17]

All discussion on trade between India and Pakistan is limited by a host of factors which makes conclusive analysis difficult. Firstly, no one really knows how much of unofficial (smuggled) and third-country trade actually takes place, so even the figures of $1-1.5 billion are open to debate; we really don't know. Secondly, and perhaps more importantly, much of the analysis on improving trade relations between the two countries is based on a *static* analysis which is based on the very limited *existing* trade patterns. No one really knows the true potential of trade between India and Pakistan because so far most of the trade has been in a very small handful of commodities.

Free 'normal' trade between India and Pakistan would allow thousands of goods which have so far not been traded, to come into the markets of both the countries. For example, the talk about two pipe and gas lines from Turkmenistan and Iran to India resulting in gains to both Pakistan and India may materialise once talks resume and political conditions improve. Although it is difficult to say how much Pakistan would gain from royalties and by laying the pipelines, royalty figures – though unreliable – are being quoted at $500 million each year for each of the pipelines. If these figures are true, they could eventually be equivalent to as much as 8-12 percent of Pakistan's export earnings – not a figure to scoff at.

---

17. Ibid.

Moreover, with lower transportation costs, there is likely to be some import 'switching' as well, where goods previously imported from other countries may now be imported from India. Trade between India and Pakistan will bring down the cost of business (particularly for Pakistan), enhance the purchasing power of consumers and increase government revenue. The volume and variety of tradable goods, given a period of time, can be extraordinary. In addition, in keeping with developments at the SAARC level where SAFTA is to come into effect within two years, the overall trade climate in South Asia will change for the better. It is also possible that while SAFTA-related developments enhance the overall trade exchange in South Asia as a whole, Pakistan and India can begin to trade more actively ahead and beyond the confines of SAFTA.

If there is a difference between where India finds itself in 2004 and where Pakistan finds itself, it lies in the fact that India's future economic prospects are no longer as critically dependent on improved political and economic relations with Pakistan as Pakistan's appear to be with India. It would be fair to say that neither South Asia nor Pakistan are any longer critical to India's future growth and well-being, as relations with India and the region still seem to be for Pakistan. However, it is true that regional economic integration and political stability and peace in South Asia can serve both India and Pakistan well in meeting their respective development objectives.[18]

18. I am grateful to Sanjaya Baru for this observation.

Recent Macro-economic Developments: 1998-2004

The first sentence of the Pakistan Economic Survey 1998-99 of the Government of Pakistan, released in June 1999, states that 'the outgoing fiscal year 1998-99 has been the most difficult and challenging year for Pakistan's economy'.[1] The Annual Report of the State Bank of Pakistan for 1998-99, released in December 1999 under radically different circumstances, concurs and begins with almost exactly the same statement: 'The year 1998-99 was one of the most difficult years in the history of Pakistan'.[2] Not only was the analysis of the past year in both these documents interesting given the numerous political developments that had taken place in Pakistan during the course of the fiscal year (which

---

1. Government of Pakistan, *Pakistan Economic Survey 1998-99*, Islamabad, 1999, p. vii.
2. State Bank of Pakistan, *Annual Report 1998-99*, Karachi, 1999, p. 1.

ran from July 1998 to June 1999), but what was even more interesting was that in the space of the six months in which these two reports were released (June and December), the government which was responsible for the first document (the Pakistan Economic Survey), had been forcibly removed from office through a military coup, and the second document (the State Bank Annual Report), was produced by a completely different set of people. Yet both concurred that the period 1998-99 was the 'most difficult year for Pakistan's economy'.

Almost each and every one of the years in the six year period 1998-2004 has been quite critical and meaningful, if not quite dramatic, in the context of the political and economic developments within Pakistan and also internationally, which subsequently had a major impact on the country. This section looks at the economic consequences of numerous such political and diplomatic events. For the most part, despite the numerous changes in governments since 1988, the economic policies followed were those of the IMF and World Bank and were quite similar. In the period after 1998, the economic policies continued on the IMF/World Bank path, but were further enforced and deepened, especially after General Musharraf took over in October 1999, with a new economic team comprising bureaucrats and bankers from the World Bank, IMF and Citibank. However, due to the nature of the non-economic developments in the period after 1998, extraneous developments have also had a very significant bearing on economic developments in the country.

Despite the fact that in each of these six years, there have been one or two quite significant developments, we do not discuss each year separately. Rather, we look at some of the important issues, processes and developments that have taken place in the economy on account of numerous events. We examine the impact of nuclear tests, of 9/11 and its consequences, the debt crisis and debt rescheduling, the increase in foreign exchange reserves, and other issues including the question of stabilisation and growth. However, before we examine the developments after 1998, it would be useful to quickly get a picture of the state of the economy prior to this period, particularly during the 1990s, and then examine subsequent events in the light of earlier trends.

Before and After May 1998

Although both the State Bank of Pakistan Annual Report of 1998-99 and the Pakistan Economic Review of the same year believe that this year was one of the most 'difficult' in Pakistan's history, it was certainly not one of the worst, in terms of economic outcomes. In fact, as Table 14 shows, in terms of GDP growth, 1998-99 was far better than the two previous years and the three subsequent years, although no one will deny that after 1998, the situation did deteriorate on account of the developments of 1998. In fact, the growth rate for 1998-99 was only marginally lower than the average for the preceding eight years, 1990-98.

Table 14: Key Economic Indicators 1990-2003

	GDP growth rate	Agri growth rate	Manufacturing growth rate	Growth rates in Total Investment	Inflation CPI	Fiscal Deficit (% of GDP)	Growth in Exports	Pop. below Poverty Line	Remittances in US $ million	Fixed Investment as % GDP
1980s avg	6.5	5.4	8.2		7.2	7.1	8.5	17.32*		17.0
1990/91	5.6	5.0	6.3	19.4	12.7	8.8	19.8	22.11	1,848	17.4
1991/92	7.7	9.5	8.1	26.2	10.6	7.5	14.6		1,467	18.5
1992/93	2.1	-5.3	4.4	13.8	9.8	8.1	0.3		1,562	19.1
1993/94	4.4	5.2	4.5	10.0	11.3	5.9	-1.4		1,445	17.9
1994/95	5.1	6.6	2.5	13.4	13.0	5.6	16.1		1,866	16.9
1995/96	6.6	11.7	3.7	16.4	10.8	6.5	7.1		1,416	17.2
1996/97	1.7	0.1	-0.1	8.0	11.8	6.4	-2.6	31.00	1,409	16.2
1997/98	3.5	4.5	6.9	9.0	7.8	7.7	4.2		1,489	14.7
1998/99	4.2	1.9	4.1	-3.6	5.7	6.1	-10.7		1,061	13.9
1999/00	3.9	6.1	1.5	10.2	3.6	6.6	8.8		983	14.4
2000/01	2.2	-2.7	8.2	5.5	4.4	5.2	9.1	32.60	1,086	13.9
2001/02	3.4	-0.1	5.0	0.4	3.5	5.2	2.3		2,389	13.1
2002/03	5.1	4.1	7.7	16.2	3.3	4.6	16.6		4,236	13.1

Note:* This data is for 1986/87.

Source: Government of Pakistan, *Pakistan Economic Survey*, various issues, Islamabad, and State Bank of Pakistan, *Annual Reports*, various issues, Karachi.

While the nuclear tests of May 1998 did have major consequences for the economy, as we will discuss later, the economy prior to 1998 cannot be claimed to have been doing very much better. In fact, as we argue earlier, the nineties as a whole were the decade of an under-developing Pakistan, especially compared to the 1980s. This, we argue, was on account of the policies implemented on the advice of the IMF and the World Bank, especially at a time when the debt overhang from the 1980s had become quite severe. Not only were the policies of the IMF and the World Bank quite disastrous, but the way they were implemented by different governments, the timing, sequencing and speed of the reforms were also responsible for the poor performance of the decade of the 1990s. Nevertheless, given its importance, the question as to why the 1990s were so bad and why there was an economic decline needs to be addressed.

Clearly, one reason was the continuous change in governments during the 1990s. The fact that there were eleven governments in as many years between 1988-99 surely cannot bode well for any developing country, especially when there was considerable antagonism between the different regimes trying to undo any project or initiative undertaken by their predecessors. The lack of stability and continuity in how policies were to be implemented, gave rise to a lack of investor confidence. The suspicion that Pakistan had nuclear weapons in the early 1990s resulted in the imposition of the Pressler Amendment which restricted US assistance to Pakistan. With debt reaching close to 100 percent of the GDP and with interest payments constituting 60 percent of the budget each year – and defence taking another 25 percent – there was very little left for development. As a consequence, there was a fall in new infrastructure investment and overall, as public sector investment contracted, so did private investment. With the IMF/World Bank conditionality of having to reduce Pakistan's fiscal deficit being paramount and with defence spending and interest payments irreducible, the axe fell on development expenditure.

Added to all this, was the severely deteriorating law and order situation in Karachi, Pakistan's main economic and financial centre, which surely made matters far worse. The economic costs and implications of Pakistanis carrying out *jihad* in different parts of the region and globe, perhaps even supported by state institutions, and the rise of religious fundamentalist forces, gave Pakistan an image which would not have been very favourable for attracting foreign (or even local) investors. Pakistan's image problem persists till today. Nevertheless, the May 1998 nuclear tests did have a major impact on events, but as it has happened so many times in Pakistan's history, soon after, other events turned out to be quite fortuitous for the country, and helped in wiping out somewhat the losses incurred as a consequence of the nuclear tests.

Soon after the nuclear tests, the developed countries – the G-7 – imposed a wide range of economic sanctions on Pakistan. The Japanese, for example, having experienced the outcome of nuclear lunacy, do not do business with any country which conducts nuclear tests. As a consequence, the Japanese government stopped all funding of projects and aid, both to India and to Pakistan. Other governments also castigated Pakistan (more so than India, which was also on the firing line) for undertaking the tests and cut aid and assistance on which the Pakistani economy and government had become most dependent. The IMF also suspended its ESAF and Extended Fund Facility programmes as well as new Official Development Assistance. On all accounts, Pakistan was squeezed by western donors and governments as a consequence of undertaking these nuclear tests. The State Bank of Pakistan Annual Report for 1997/98 summarised the issues as follows:

> Developments in May, 1998 had a major impact on balance of payments, net foreign assets of the banking system, stock market and the exchange rate. The nuclear blast by India immediately affected the investors' confidence and the stock market declined, free market exchange rate depreciated, and foreign currency deposits were withdrawn significantly during May 11-28, 1998. Pakistan's response on May 28, 1998 to the Indian detonation, followed by economic sanctions by the United States, and a restraining stance adopted by the G-7 countries with regard to the lending by the international financial institutions, further contributed towards the erosion of confidence and weakening of the budget and the balance of payments.[3]

Nevertheless, one specific action by the Government of Pakistan was probably more responsible for setting off a domino effect than anything else.

While the nuclear tests were bad enough, the freeze on Foreign Currency Accounts (FCAs) soon after made matters far worse and caused major problems. Since January 1973, Pakistanis living abroad holding certain types of foreign currencies were allowed to open bank accounts in Pakistan. The purpose of this scheme was to allow the government to

3. State Bank of Pakistan, *Annual Report 1997-98*, Karachi, 1998, p. 2.

capture some of the vast amount of foreign exchange earned and held by the large number of Pakistanis working abroad. In 1991, even resident Pakistanis were allowed this privilege, and many bought dollars and other currencies and deposited them in Pakistani banks in Pakistan. Pakistan has a large underground/black/illegal sector, and it is estimated that at least 40-80 percent of its GDP equivalent is held in the black economy. An additional assumption is that many Pakistanis have promoted the flight of capital by keeping legal and illegal income abroad.

In order to address these issues and attempt to reverse capital flight, governments in Pakistan encouraged resident Pakistanis to keep foreign currency at home. This led to the speculation of foreign currencies and to the 'dollarisation' of the economy, where anyone who had any illegal or ill-gotten wealth, immediately purchased dollars and deposited it into their resident FCAs. This quest for dollars kept a constant pressure on the exchange rate, pushing it up to artificially high levels, causing the rupee to be devalued, which had numerous other repercussions on the economy. The rates of return on foreign currency deposits were exempt from income tax and *zakaat*, and were 'considerably higher than for rupee financial assets ... and this has been one of the most important factors leading to dollarization'.[4] Add to this the high inflation prevalent in Pakistan at that time and the steady depreciation of the rupee, and you have an asset which would have been secure and guaranteed higher returns than any other. Perhaps

4. Ibid., p. 116.

that is why, by May 1998, around $11 billion had been deposited into Pakistani banks by resident and non-resident Pakistanis.

The Indian nuclear tests were undertaken on May 11 and until May 28 when Pakistan tested its own, some foreign currency was withdrawn. Fearing a run on the rupee, and that Pakistanis would rush to withdraw their deposits, the government of Nawaz Sharif put a freeze on withdrawals, not allowing the deposit holders to withdraw their own money. The government justified this action as follows: 'The past experience had shown that in a period of uncertainty, foreign currency deposits begin to be withdrawn and it was apprehended that it could take place on a large scale and sustained basis in the post May 28 period'.[5] This caused what is for sure Pakistan's greatest crisis of confidence, and all the trust that had been accumulated over many years, evaporated as a result of this one gesture.

It was probably this measure, more than any other, which made Nawaz Sharif's government very unpopular. Perhaps his government over-reacted and should have had some more confidence in its policies and promises, but it seems, after all, that the cupboard was bare. The government knew that the actual level of foreign exchange reserves was much lower than the $11 billion it should have had, and had the run taken place, would not have been able to meet its liabilities. The consequence of imposing the freeze was that in six weeks, at the end of the fiscal year in June, the stock market was down by 37.6

5. Ibid. p. 2.

percent, and more importantly, the free market exchange rate had depreciated by 16.2 percent and liquid foreign exchange reserves had declined to only $423 million, a fraction of the liabilities.

The crisis of confidence had a particularly strong impact on investors, both local and foreign, and with sanctions imposed, and credit ratings very low, the general trend was most unfavourable for the economy. Even a government which had real, liquid, foreign exchange in cash worth $11 billion, as the government in 2004 does, would probably not initiate a scheme allowing residents to open Foreign Currency Accounts. More importantly, even if the government were to announce such a scheme now, it is improbable that there would be many takers. Trust once lost, in this case even through the hands of an earlier government, is very difficult to regain.

September 11, 2001: The Day the World Changed

After May 1998, when it became clear that Pakistan had nuclear capability, a known secret since at least 1986, Pakistan, not so much India, became a pariah state. While sanctions continued and as Table 14 shows, the economy after 1998 slowed down, numerous developments in 1999 made that year one of the most remarkable in Pakistan's 57-year history.

In February 1999, Indian Prime Minister Atal Behari Vajpayee made what at that time was thought to be a historic trip to Lahore and with the Prime Minister of Pakistan, Nawaz Sharif, signed the Lahore Declaration, trying to take both countries, now open and acknowledged nuclear states, towards the road to peace. Prospects of trade and better relations seemed to be on the horizon, but more importantly, there was a feeling that perhaps peace would become a priority for both nations. However, the peace process was quickly derailed by the Pakistan military's huge misadventure in Kargil, which cost both Pakistan and India not just many hundreds of lives, but also destroyed any hope for peace and wrecked the trust that had been built up just a few weeks earlier.

While the first half of 1999 consisted of these two extremes of peace and war, in October 1999, the democratically elected government of Nawaz Sharif was dismissed by General Musharraf in Pakistan's third coup. As it is, Pakistan was being considered a rogue state for testing its nuclear devices, and the re-entry of the military into government after a lapse of eleven years, did not improve Pakistan's image at first. Some further sanctions were imposed on the country, and as Table 14 shows, the economy was staggering. However, all that changed after 9/11.

Pakistan had enough political and economic problems as it was, prior to 9/11. The nuclear test-related sanctions were still in place, democracy had been overthrown by a military coup, Pakistan's debt burden was still huge – see below – and as Table 14 shows, the downturn in the economy had already set in prior to 9/11. There were two sets of major factors from 9/11 which were related to Pakistan's economic future.

The first set included issues which emerged as a response to the world economic growth slowing down more generally. This meant that with world growth slowing down, so would the demand for exports from the developed markets. Consumption and incomes fell in developed countries, and so did imports from other countries. Moreover, there was a sense of shock and insecurity, which meant that Americans were less enthusiastic to spend and were holding back. Second, there was a huge fear of Muslims, Islam, and people from other – particularly Middle Eastern – countries. Pakistan was also included in this category, so most US businesses and firms treated Pakistanis and Pakistan with distrust, if not contempt. This meant that foreign investors would not be willing to invest in Pakistan nor even visit possible exporters and markets in the country. Travel advisories were issued which persuaded US and other western businessmen not to visit places like Pakistan.

Moreover, with the US bombardment of Afghanistan in order to annihilate members of the Taliban regime, in which Pakistan played a key role, Pakistan became the backyard of the US' war against terror and its war in Afghanistan. The backlash was that many suspected al-Qaeda members and former Taliban members found refuge in Pakistan, causing Pakistan to be further blacklisted, if at all that could have been possible.[6] By all accounts, Pakistan was a no-go area for foreigners, particularly Americans, whether they were donors

---

6. For the political and economic consequences of the US war against Afghanistan, and with particular reference to the developments in Pakistan's politics, see many of the essays in Zaidi, S. Akbar, *Continuity and Change: Socio-Political and Institutional Dynamics*, City Press, Karachi, 2003.

or businessmen. In addition, many countries were no longer eager to deal with Pakistani businessmen and industry suffered. However, as Pakistan once again became a front-line state, things changed once again, this time very fortuitously.

Even with the Government of Pakistan very quickly throwing in its lot with the Americans in their war against Afghanistan, and in the worldwide war against terror, the immediate negative costs and complications were those listed above, many of which continue to this day. Nevertheless, in the medium and longer term, things changed dramatically, particularly for the military government of General Musharraf. From being labelled a rogue Islamic military state with nuclear pretensions, General Musharraf was welcomed back into the comity of civilised nations fighting the war against terror. Overnight, he became the darling of the West, with dozens of leaders and dignitaries from the developed countries – the very same leaders who had denounced his coup two years earlier – visiting him in Islamabad. While this ensured his political longevity at least for some time, the economic returns of siding with the Americans were unprecedented.

The biggest problem that had plagued Pakistan's government for many years since the profligate 1980s under General Zia, was that of excessive and growing debt (both domestic and international, but particularly the latter) and annual interest payments. Pakistan's economy was struggling under debt equivalent to its GDP, with half of it being foreign debt. As a return for Pakistan's support to the US in particular and the West in general, huge amounts of debt were either written off, or rescheduled under very easy and comfortable terms, relieving the pressure on Pakistan's foreign exchange situation. In addition, the quota for Pakistani exports to the US and the European Union was increased to compensate for earlier cancelled orders.

Equally important was the signal to the IMF and the World Bank and numerous other donors, to re-enter the field and begin supporting Pakistan again. For example, even USAID returned to Pakistan after nearly a decade, an aid agency which had exited Pakistan once nuclear-related sanctions were enforced under the Pressler Amendment in the early 1990s. Pakistan was no longer no-go territory, and as a consequence of Pakistan's role in the war against terror and war against Afghanistan (and subsequently, in the US' war against Iraq later in 2003) Pakistan's government was repaid handsomely. Another consequence was the huge increase in remittances, particularly from the US, which came to Pakistan, particularly in 2002-03 – see below.

One needs to emphasise that, *had the New York attack not taken place, it is quite improbable that Pakistan would have been able to get out of the post-nuclear tests and post-military coup scenario, both of which had been damaging to the economy.* If one takes the narrow view of merely looking at the short-term economic aspects, then the dividends from Pakistan's support to the US have been very high. However, this is a very narrow, opportunistic view which has had, and is bound to have, numerous other (probably negative) consequences in the longer term.

What Happened to the Debt Crisis?

Even a cursory reading of any government document or academic study by economists at any time during the 1990s, immediately reveals that Pakistan was faced with a 'crippling', 'devastating' debt crisis for the entire duration of that decade. Both external and domestic debt had reached astronomical, unsustainable levels, as had the budget deficit and interest payments which continued to give rise to further debt, both domestic and foreign. Add to this the fact that the economy was doing particularly poorly in terms of investment, growth and revenue generation, and one can understand the nature of a real and growing economic crisis.

The external debt and interest payments had reached such astronomical proportions (see tables below) that there was a real fear that Pakistan would default on its international commitments and be declared bankrupt, in addition to being called a rogue or pariah state. However, in December 2001, but more specifically by 2002, the external debt crisis had become, for the moment at least, forgotten and 'resolved', and in fiscal year 2003-04, the government of Pakistan had even voluntarily retired $1.2 billion before its due date. How did this dramatic turnaround take place?

In order to gauge the extent of the crisis and the gravity of the situation, it is important to know the amount of external debt owed and interest payments being made each year. Table 15 presents key ratios and data which give a clear picture.

Table 15 shows that by 1998-99, external debt was more than half the size of the GDP, and with domestic debt around

Table 15: Pakistan's External Debt Outstanding and Servicing – (Old Format) in million dollars

	Total Debt Outstanding	Growth Rates (in per cent)	Annual Debt Servicing	Growth Rates (in per cent)	Outstanding Debt as per cent of GDP	Debt Servicing as per cent of Export Earnings	Debt Servicing as per cent of Foreign Exchange Earnings
1993-94	24,482	11.0	3,612	22.7	47.6	54.0	33.4
1994-95	25,318	3.4	4,324	19.7	41.7	55.7	34.9
1995-96	27,094	7.0	4,347	0.5	44.3	52.3	33.9
1996-97	27,863	2.8	5,083	16.9	44.7	62.8	39.3
1997-98	28,682	6.0	4,670	-8.1	48.4	55.4	34.9
1998-99	30,328	5.7	2,644	-43.4	51.7	34.9	23.0

Source: State Bank of Pakistan, *Annual Report 1999-2000*, Karachi, 2000.

the same amount as well, Pakistan's total domestic and external debt was greater than the size of the GDP. While Pakistan was paying back around a third in export earnings in the form of debt servicing, it was still adding on to the stock of overall total external debt. Clearly, this trend was not particularly helpful for Pakistan's economy, and is one of the reasons for the very poor economic growth and social statistics during the 1990s.

Table 16 only endorses the view based on the earlier table, perhaps more forcefully, that Pakistan's external debt crisis had become quite serious in the mid-1990s. The total external debt to GDP ratio was the highest in the fateful year 1998-99 after the nuclear tests and their repercussions, and with Foreign Currency Accounts very substantial, the total external liabilities to GDP ratio was also very high in that year and in the years preceding it. Most figures and ratios seem to have peaked in 1998/99 after which there is a noticeable improvement. One reason was that some initial debt rescheduling began to take place in 1999, but the main reason, probably, was that it was in October 1999 when General Musharraf took over Pakistan's government with a new

Table 16: Selected External Debt and External Liabilities Indicators

	TED $ mn	TEL $ mn	TED to GDP %	TED to EE %	TED to FEE %	TEL to GDP %	TEL to EE %	TEL to FEE %	DS/XGS %	RES/TEL
1980-81			35.0	360.3						
1984-85			39.2	486.1						
1989-90			52.6	414.2						
1994-95			47.7	371.4	232.9	61.4	479.0	300.3		
1995-96			47.1	358.3	232.2	61.6	695.9	451.0		
1996-97			48.4	372.6	233.4	68.0	523.3	327.7		
1997-98	32,080	33,840	48.5	356.5	224.9	53.7	394.7	249.1	46.0	2.8
1998-99	32,864	36,600	57.4	446.4	298.9	66.4	517.0	346.2	29.7	4.4
1999-00	32,254	37,918	53.1	395.1	252.9	62.4	464.5	297.3	31.6	3.6
2000-01	32,161	37,177	54.9	360.0	224.3	63.6	416.2	259.3	32.7	5.6
2001-02	33,400	36,532	56.6	365.7	216.1	62.1	400.0	236.4	36.7	13.2
2002-03	33,352	35,474	48.5	364.7	171.8	51.6	387.9	182.7	22.8	28.2

Note: TED: Total external debt; TEL: Total external liabilities, which includes TED; EE: Export earnings; FEE: Foreign exchange earnings; DS: Debt servicing; XGS: Exports of goods and services.

Source: Data for 1997/98 to 2002/03 is from the State Bank of Pakistan, *Annual Report 2002-03*, Karachi, 2003, p. 135; for 1994/95 to 1996/97, from the State Bank of Pakistan, *Annual Report 2001-02*, Karachi, 2002, p. 143; and for the earlier years and for the averages, from State Bank of Pakistan, *Annual Report 2001-02*, Karachi, 2002, p. 150.

team of economic and finance managers. Did the reversal in the trends come about because of better management or were there other factors involved?

Pakistan has been allowed to reschedule debt on numerous occasions in the past, as Table 17 shows. However, the scale of rescheduling in more recent years, particularly in December 2001, largely as a payback to General Musharraf for the role he has played in supporting the US in their war against Afghanistan, has been extraordinary.

Table 17: Amount of Debt Rescheduling in Pakistan ($ million)

1971-73	233.766
1973-74	107.166
1974-78	650.0
1977-78	226.303
1980-82	232.0
1985-88	11.0
1998-99	1987.63
1999-00	1241.70
2000-01	617.28
December 2001	12,500.00

Source: Siddiqui R. and R. Siddiqui, 'Determinants of Debt Rescheduling in Pakistan', *The Pakistan Development Review*, Vol. 40, No. 4, Part II, 2001, p. 694

In January 1999, following the foreign exchange problems that had been initiated after Pakistan's nuclear tests and the freeze on Foreign Currency Accounts and the refusal of many donors to lend to Pakistan, the Nawaz Sharif government approached the Paris Club members to reschedule its public and publicly guaranteed debt. The Paris Club agreed to reschedule some of the debt service payments due for the period January 1, 1999 to December 31, 2000 in respect of the loans which were contracted prior to September 30, 1997. Once the Paris Club agreed to reschedule the $2.744 billion repayments, the government also got some relief from non-Paris Club bilateral creditors, and ended up getting rescheduling worth $3.1 billion in this period. It was the return of the IMF to Pakistan in the guise of yet another agreement in January 1999 which allowed the rescheduling to proceed. At the end of the first consolidation period in December 2000, another round of rescheduling was sought from sovereign and commercial creditors. With the new Musharraf government in place, a Stand By Agreement with the IMF was reached in November 2000, and in January 2001, the Paris Club and other bilateral and commercial creditors agreed to restructure debts worth $ 1.8 billion.

However, the earlier debt rescheduling was minuscule compared to the $12.5 billion that was rescheduled in December 2001. Not only was this amount far larger than any such rescheduling in the past, more importantly, it was the terms of this agreement which set it apart. As the State Bank Annual Report states, 'The Paris Club offered very generous terms; in contrast to the previous two rescheduling agreements that provided relief *only* in terms of debt flows[7] (as per

7. This 'flow' rescheduling limits rescheduling to the debt servicing (principal plus interest) falling due within a specified period – the consolidation period – which usually coincides with a country's programme with the IMF. This flow rescheduling provides temporary relief, as after the consolidation period, the magnitude of debt servicing reverts to the former high level. The issue of 'debt overhang' is only deferred, not resolved.

Houston terms), the existing arrangement is applicable to the entire stock of US $12.5 billion of Pakistan's bilateral debt owed to the Paris Club creditors. Consequently, this provided an implied debt reduction without having a HIPC [Heavily Indebted Poor Country] status, which is generally associated with *Naples* terms'.[8]

Basically, the entire bilateral debt of consortium countries has been rescheduled, and this rescheduling has been for a far greater period than in the past. Official Development Assistance (ODA) debt, which is 68 percent of the total rescheduled, will be repayable after 35 years, with a 15-year grace period, and non-ODA debt is to be repaid over a 25 year period, with a five year grace period for other loans. Moreover, there has been a 're-profiling of the debt in such a way that it takes into consideration the country's capacity to pay'.[9] This rescheduling allows relief of between $1.2-1.5 billion annually in the debt servicing payments on external debt during the years 2001-05.[10] Add to this the favourable fact that Pakistan has not just had a debt rescheduling, but an actual *debt write-off* by many

---

8. State Bank of Pakistan, *Annual Report 2001-02*, Karachi, 2002, p. 147, emphasis in original; the Report also states in a footnote that this is 'beneficial for Pakistan as HIPC status restricts borrowing on normal terms from IBRD, ADB or market sources'. In other words, while not being an HIPC, Pakistan has been allowed the same privileges.
9. Kemal, A.R., 'Debt Accumulation and its Implications for Growth and Poverty' *The Pakistan Development Review*, Vol. 40, No. 4, Part II, 2001, p. 272.
10. For further details see Government of Pakistan, *Pakistan Economic Survey 2002-03*, Islamabad, 2003, pp 152-154.

friendly countries; we are in an extraordinarily fortuitous situation based on Pakistan's support for the US invasion of Afghanistan.[11]

Despite this considerable rescheduling, it is important to emphasise that Pakistan is still making substantial payments in the form of debt servicing to its creditors, as Table 18 shows. In 2001-02, Pakistan paid as much as $6.3 billion, equivalent to more than half its export earnings.

Table 18: Pakistan's External Debt and Liabilities Servicing (New Format) $ million

	Actual paid	Rescheduled
1999/00	3,756	4,081
2000/01	5,101	2,795
2001/02	6,327	2,243
2002/03p	4,301	1,908

p: provisional
Source: State Bank of Pakistan, *Annual Reports*, various issues, Karachi.

Sakib Sherani argues that due to the factors highlighted above (also due to an increase in foreign exchange reserves) 'the acute vulnerability associated with its [Pakistan's] account for much of the 1990s has dissipated significantly. This appears to be providing the catalyst for a significant reversal of the

11. By June 2003, $1.062 billion worth of debt had been cancelled/ written-off largely by the US, which wrote-off $1 billion of this total.

systemic outflows of private capital experienced in the previous decade. This phenomenon, in conjunction with substantially enhanced levels of official inflows ... the restructuring of debt provid[ing] for reduction of at least 30 percent in the net present value of the eligible debt stock ... is expected to effect a significant improvement in Pakistan's debt situation in the medium term'.[12] He adds that barring any significant unanticipated deviations, 'Pakistan's external public debt will approach sustainable levels by FY2007 [2006-07].'[13]

The Growing Forex Reserves

While Pakistan's debt situation has improved considerably over the last three years, so have the country's foreign exchange reserves. In 1999-2000 Pakistan's total forex reserves were $2.77 billion, but rose to $7.07 billion at the end of fiscal year 2001-02, and by the next year in June 2003, were $11.48 billion, and were expected to rise even further. Moreover, in 2003-04, the Government of Pakistan was able to retire some of its foreign debt to the tune of $1 billion. While the substantial increase in foreign exchange reserves has allowed Pakistan's international credit rating to improve, allowing further private and public inflows, the most important consequence has been

12. Sherani, Sakib, *Escaping the Debt Trap: An Assessment of Pakistan's External Debt Sustainability*, Asian Development Bank, Pakistan Resident Mission Working Paper Series No 1, Islamabad, December 2002, p. 71.
13. Ibid., p. 72.

the stabilisation and in fact appreciation, of the Pakistani rupee. In 2001-02, the average US $/Pakistan Rupee rate was $1 equal to Rs 61.43, which had improved to Rs 58.50 by the end of the next fiscal year. Moreover, the difference between the official and market rates, which had always been higher, had more or less disappeared, bringing both rates in line. Clearly, compared to a near bankrupt Pakistan in 1998-99, much had changed.

There have been two or three factors which have resulted in an unprecedented growth in foreign exchange reserves, showing an increase of a quite phenomenal 120 percent within one year: between 2001-02 and 2002-03 the State Bank of Pakistan's reserves rose from $4.33 billion to $9.52 billion. One factor has been an increase in Pakistan's exports, which crossed $10 billion for the first time ever in 2002-03. With a rebound of the global economy and with greater access to European and US markets with quotas being increased, this was likely to happen and continue. A second important reason has been the State Bank's purchase of foreign currency from the kerb market. The State Bank has become one of the most important buyers of foreign exchange, and has bought substantial amounts in the years since 1999-2000. Thirdly, with debt rescheduling, interest payments have also been reduced, allowing the State Bank to hold on to and increase its reserves.

It is important to point out that the more reliable and traditional forms of inflows, such as foreign direct investment, have had absolutely no significant impact on increasing foreign exchange reserves, as they have in many other countries.

Perhaps this is a matter of concern regarding the sustainability of the increase in foreign exchange reserves, if we consider the main cause for the substantial increase, especially in the last two fiscal years.

Remittances have been a reliable source of foreign exchange earnings for Pakistan since the late 1970s. In the 1980s, particularly, remittances rose to very substantial levels equivalent to around 7 or 8 percent of GDP in single years. However, since the early 1990s, and after the first Gulf War and due to structural shifts in labour demand in the Gulf States, remittances fell substantially (see Table 14). Traditionally, the Gulf States have been the main sources of remittances into Pakistan. Saudi Arabia sent between 35-45 percent of remittances in the 1990s, the UAE about 17 percent in 1999-2000 and Kuwait 15 percent in 1999-2000; Britain provided about eight percent of total remittances, and the US a maximum of 13 percent in 1996-97, which had begun to fall thereafter, and was 8.75 percent in 1999-2000. However, following 9/11 there was a dramatic change in both the volume and composition of remittances.

In 2002-03, the Pakistanis in the US sent in $1.7237 billion, which was *fifteen times* the amount sent from the US just three years ago, in 1999-2000! This trend of substantially increased remittances from the US had begun in 2001-02, with $778 million sent, which was ten times higher than the paltry $79 million sent in 1999-2000. In 2002-03, the US with this substantially increased amount of remittances now provided as much as 29.53 percent of remittances of the $4.236 billion total, the highest amount ever received by

Pakistan. Another significant development was that in 2002-03, Saudi Arabia's contribution had fallen markedly: from providing almost half Pakistan's total in the past, now Saudi Arabia provided a mere 13 percent.

The reasons for this unprecedented amount sent by Pakistanis from the US followed by Pakistanis in the UAE (20 percent of total remittances in 2002-03), was a result purely of the post-9/11 developments. The US government started scrutinising the accounts of Pakistanis and Muslims in the US, while investigating the funding for al-Qaeda type organisations. In order to avoid such investigations and fearing that their savings would be jeopardised, many Pakistanis sent back money to Pakistan which they would have preferred to keep in the US. The same sort of scrutiny had also begun in the UAE, and hence the increase in remittances from there.

Moreover, the informal foreign exchange transfer mechanism, the *hundi*, which has been responsible for the main share of remittances to Pakistan from the Middle East, also came under scrutiny. To appear legal and to avoid complications with the authorities, many Pakistanis sent back money through the formal banking sector. Also, it must be added that the State Bank of Pakistan and its commercial banks also took additional measures to capture the *hundi* market and since the differential between the official and market exchange rates had been largely eliminated, they were able to divert some funds away from the *hundi* market. Nevertheless, the main reason for this huge surge in remittances was 9/11-related developments.

Has there Been a Turnaround of the Economy?

With growth rates of 5.1 percent in 2002-03 and 6.4 percent in 2003-04 being at their highest levels since 1995-96, with the inflation rate down to its lowest in almost fifteen years, with the fiscal deficit at its lowest in almost two decades, with remittances at their highest levels ever, with exports crossing the $12 billion mark for the first time and showing signs of further growth, the government is claiming that the economy has rebounded, that there has been a 'turnaround' and that good times have returned. Even the stock market has soared to inconceivable levels, setting new records every week. We are finally out of the ruinous decade of the 1990s and set on course for growth and development.

There is no disagreement over the claim that the economy has done far better in the last two or three years, since 2000-01, than it has for many years. In fact, one can add that it is very probable that this trend will continue into the next two or three years as well. The growth rate is likely to be above 5 percent for the next few years, exports will probably not fall below the $12 billion mark, and with substantial fiscal space created on account of the rescheduling done by the Paris Club, the pressure on the economy, at least for a few years, has been eased. There is also no denying the fact that this change has taken place on account of the developments globally, and also particularly in the region, on account of 9/11. What is most questionable, however, is the claim that Pakistan is out of the woods, and headed for *sustained* development and growth.

The reasons for this scepticism rest on a number of factors. One reason is that the recovery that has taken place in Pakistan has been on the back of high remittances, which are likely to subside to far lower levels than those in the fiscal year 2002-03. This means that the additional foreign exchange reserves are likely to have slower rates of increase, since remittances are a key factor causing the increase. A second reason is that once the WTO regime takes effect, with a quota-free textile world, Pakistan will be faced with greater competition and will not be allowed the privileged access it has been granted to the US and to Europe after 9/11. This may result in the growth rate of exports slowing down, leading to a possible deterioration in the much improved current account balance. Besides, with 67 percent of the exports being textiles-based, a more serious crisis may have been overlooked by the increase in exports in 2002-03.

Poverty in Pakistan continues to be a major concern, with almost a third of the population living below the poverty line. Unless GDP growth stays above the 5.5 percent level for a number of years, it is improbable that Pakistan will see much decrease in poverty levels. One of the main problems facing Pakistan is that of job creation and poverty alleviation based on active private sector investment. This is particularly important because the public sector has been withdrawing from productive activities and has been cutting down as well as privatising its assets. The government still insists on further reducing the fiscal deficit to below 4 percent of GDP, thereby restricting resources for development.

Moreover, 'in real terms, overall private fixed investment has remained virtually stagnant for much of the 1990s, while fixed investment in large-scale manufacturing has exhibited a secular declining trend during the period'.[14] Sherani continues, 'the failure to elicit an investment response from the private sector despite a significant degree of structural adjustment undertaken has been the weakest links in Pakistan's efforts to forge sustainable economic development'.[15] As Table 14 shows, investment is currently only 13 per cent of GDP, far lower than earlier trends, and probably the *lowest since the late 1950s*.

Despite efforts to attract domestic (and foreign) capital and investment, both have been reluctant to come forth and become a part of the growth trends emerging in the economy. Add to this the government's own conservatism in exploring new possibilities by being highly risk averse and relying too heavily on stabilisation rather than growth, and continuing to have mere stability, not dynamism. Furthermore, 'the mechanism for this policy [of stabilisation] has been contractionary fiscal policy, including cuts in development expenditure ... [This] has dampened investment and curtailed purchasing power, leading to a recessionary situation. It has contributed directly to the increase in unemployment and policy. That the policy continues to be pursued with greater vigour is unfortunate'.[16]

While structural weaknesses continue to plague Pakistan's economy, and will take time to be sorted out, issues of regional

---

14. Sherani, Sakib, op. cit., p. 89 (footnote 12).
15. Ibid.
16. Bengali, Kaiser and Qazi Masood Ahmed, 'Stabilisation Policy vs. Growth-oriented Policy: Implications for the Pakistan Economy'. *The Pakistan Development Review*, Vol. 40, No. 4, part II, 2001, p. 464.

and domestic political uncertainty do not ensure stability either. For example, many of the reforms undertaken and the bonhomie that Pakistan has felt in recent years, have been initiated by one individual, General Musharraf. Through his own personality and his interaction with world leaders and by making better use of a particular situation – 9/11 – he has been able to exploit considerable mileage out of world events. However, the political consequences of siding with the Americans have also had negative consequences, with General Musharraf being the target of a number of assassination attempts. What will happen if he is replaced?

Probably the greatest failure has been that of the institutions in Pakistan – democratic, bureaucratic, and civil society. Pakistan and its government and institutions have been largely individual-centric and personality-driven. What happens when individuals are replaced, is anyone's guess. However, it does not address the problem of uncertainty and the lack of continuity, which have been Pakistan's biggest problems. Moreover, Pakistan's 'image problem' still persists – as the result of harbouring al-Qaeda members and other Islamic fundamentalists, militants and jihadis – and is unlikely to go away so easily or so soon.

Clearly, it is not possible to suggest that Pakistan is out of the woods and on the road to growth, development and poverty eradication. There are too many structural weaknesses in the economy, and the fundamentals are still a long way off from being on the right track and being *sustainable*. Windfall gains and opportunistic investment do not guarantee sustainable development.

In Conclusion: The Domestic, Regional and Global Context

India has had more than five decades of a democratic process which sets it apart, not just from Pakistan, but from almost all developing countries. Pakistan, in contrast, has had a mix of military rule, with partial and still evolving forms of democracy, much of which has been administered and managed by the military itself, resulting in quasi-military/ quasi-civilian forms of government. Particularly since the last two decades from 1985 to the present, this mix-and-match of partial democracy and direct military rule have been the norm. While Pakistan's political process has been far more typical of developing countries than India's, Pakistan's present predicament is more reminiscent of an older form of government in developing countries, which is now gradually being done away with. Military rule is no longer accepted in most countries which have now moved slowly, but probably quite surely, on the road to popular democratic forms of government. Pakistan is still experimenting and evolving its own form of democracy.

Clearly, in a dispensation which has had to deal with considerable and continuous change and uncertainty at the domestic political level in just two decades – twelve governments in 17 years – the economy has suffered. Pakistan's spectacular economic performance in the 1980s stands in stark contrast to the dismal performance of the 1990s. Domestic politics has had a great deal to do with this outcome, as has the role of international financial institutions. While reforms have been – and still are – essential for Pakistan's economic development, the sequencing, timing and speed of many reforms have ended up at cross-purposes, doing far more harm than good. Interest rate liberalisation is a case in point: interest rates were freed up and allowed to rise and reflect market sentiment at a time when Pakistan was overburdened by debt. The result was that the government was contracting further debt at higher rates of interest to pay back earlier accumulated debt and its interest payments.

While politicians have borne much of the blame for Pakistan's poor performance in the 1990s, institutional and structural factors not in the control of the civilian governments, have also taken toll on the country's economy. Military spending in Pakistan continues to be almost twice the amount spent on health and education *combined*, and may offer one explanation for the rather poor state of social sector statistics cited in this book. While politicians may have been in government for much of the 1990s, much of the real power lay in the hands of non-civilian institutions. These institutions have also had a critical – determining – hand in Pakistan's regional foreign policy, which has had an impact on the economy. Clearly, not all the blame for the poor performance of the economy in the nineties can be laid at the doorstep of politicians.

Pakistan's economy benefited greatly in the 1980s as a consequence of events in Afghanistan. A great deal of aid and loans were made available to fight Soviet expansionism in the region and Pakistan became a front line state. Exactly twenty years later, it seems that history has repeated itself once again with a new war and occupant in Afghanistan. While the benefits from the first Afghan War of 1979 seemed considerable at that time, a generation later, Pakistan's society is bearing the considerable costs of state-sponsored fundamentalism abroad, but especially in Pakistan. What will be the outcome of Pakistan's current involvement in the coalition in Afghanistan, will probably be decided and evaluated much later. Nevertheless, it is not clear if at all the immediate benefits – debt rescheduling, increased market access, easier loans, etc. – will be enough to counter political forces in Pakistan which may have a very different future in mind for Pakistani society.

In many ways, Pakistan seems to be part of the global world and 'open for business'. It has lowered tariff rates, followed IMF and World Bank advice, and liberalised and opened up its economy far more than many developing countries. Pakistan seems better placed for 2005 than many other countries. Yet unlike many of the East Asian countries, it is unclear whether Pakistan will actually benefit from globalisation, despite its preparedness. A lack of investor confidence keeps investment at an all time low; poor social indicators mean that Pakistan will not have the requisite human capital or skills required to exploit the information technology and communications revolution which has been used to the advantage of many countries with an educated population; and polarisation within society and unresolved conflicts – fundamentalism, jihadis, sectarianism – have resulted in a law and order situation which is not conducive to attracting foreign (or even local) capital or investors.

Pakistan's future lies more in focusing on putting its domestic house in order and on concentrating on improving relations at the regional level. Sorting out Pakistan's continuing 'image problem' will go a long way in creating an atmosphere conducive to attracting investment and ensuring security, and can be improved by reigning in jihadis and militant groups who have a very different perspective on Pakistan's future trajectory. Better relations with India might be the answer to many of Pakistan's numerous problems. Increased regional economic and trade co-operation will benefit Pakistan tremendously, opening up a huge and expanding market in India, one that is many times the size of Pakistan's domestic market. A peace dividend will end the posturing and war-mongering of official and non-official groups, having a positive domestic impact as well. Moreover, increased integration in the region can also be seen as a counter to the threat posed by being a small country exposed to globalisation.

In order for Pakistan to have a stability which is sustainable and for it to reach a growth path of close to 6 percent per annum resulting in around 4 percent real per capita growth, a number of measures will have to be taken. Most importantly, the politics and posturing of war with India, will have to be replaced by a more active agenda for peace and cooperation. With estimates showing that as much as 45 percent of the rural population live in abject poverty, there is a need to devise a land and agrarian reform package which not only allows the poor access to land, but also allows them easy access to key inputs.

With considerable fiscal space available as a result of debt rescheduling and reprofiling, there is the possibility to increase investment in infrastructure, health and education; in the past, public sector investment has been a spur to attract private investment as the linkages between the two have been quite strong. With foreign exchange reserves considerable and breathing space available regarding domestic and foreign debt, this is as good a moment as any for the government to retire some of its high interest debt and for it to take concrete measures to raise additional revenue and address the debt problem which has been one of the main culprits for retarding economic growth in the country.

Pakistan's economy has shown considerable growth this last year, a trend that is likely to continue for a couple of years in the future. However, the foundations of this improvement have been based on rather fortuitous windfalls from extraneous factors and not so much on economic policy and intervention by economic managers. Unless structural issues are addressed, much of this temporary gain will be lost and the recovery will come undone. The answer to many of Pakistan's problems lies in reorienting its regional policy, promoting a process of peace and advancing regional integration. These measures will allow Pakistan to consolidate its recent gains and take them well into the future.

Index